AF290987

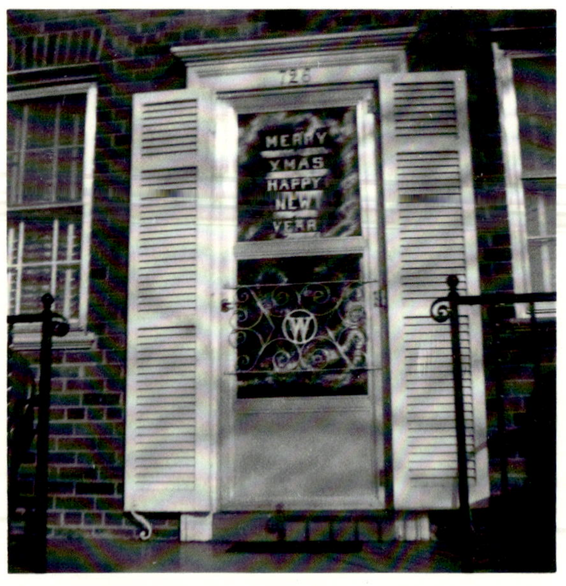

GREETINGS FROM OUR HOUSE

TO YOUR HOUSE

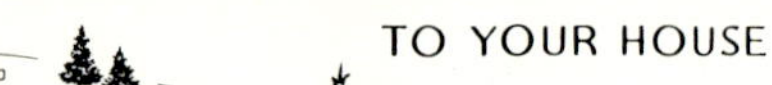

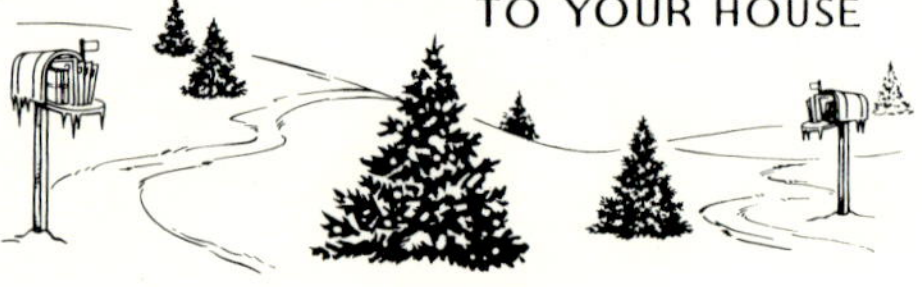

Helen and George
1960

From Our House
To Your House

Martin Parr

dewi lewis publishing

First published in the UK in 2002 by
Dewi Lewis Publishing
8 Broomfield Road
Heaton Moor
Stockport SK4 4ND
+44 (0)161 442 9450

www.dewilewispublishing.com

All cards are from the collection of Martin Parr

ISBN: 1-899235-34-5

Design & artwork production: Dewi Lewis Publishing
Print: EBS, Verona, Italy

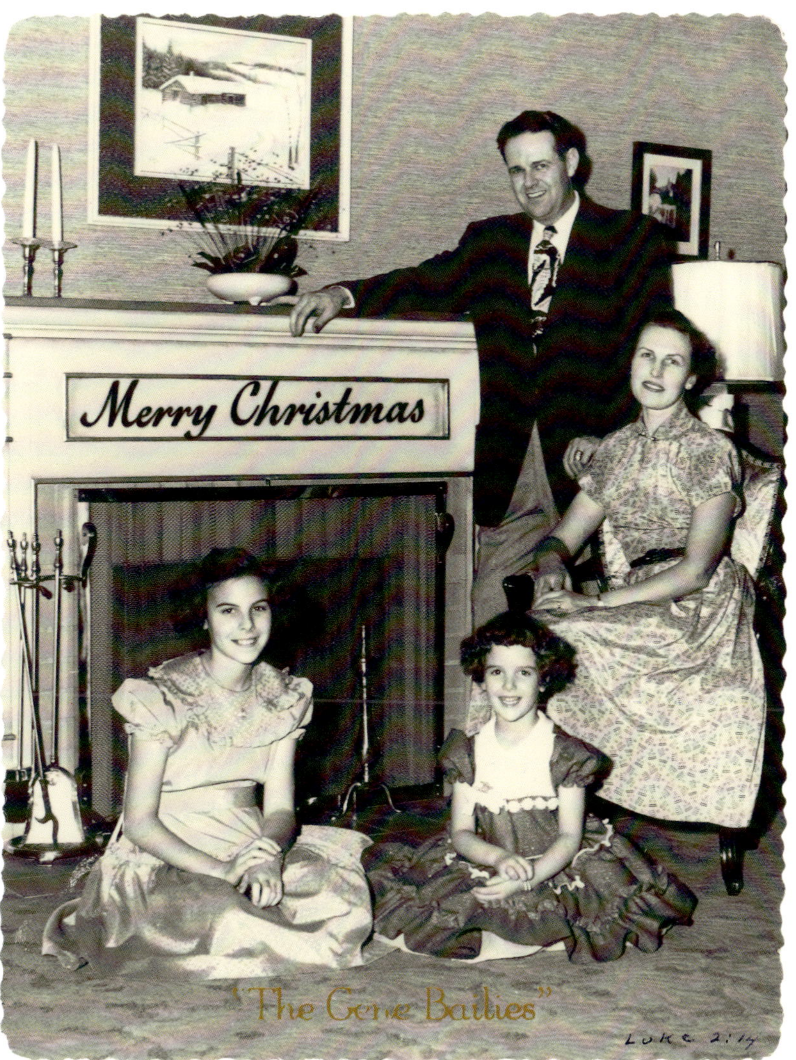
Merry Christmas
"The Gene Bailies"

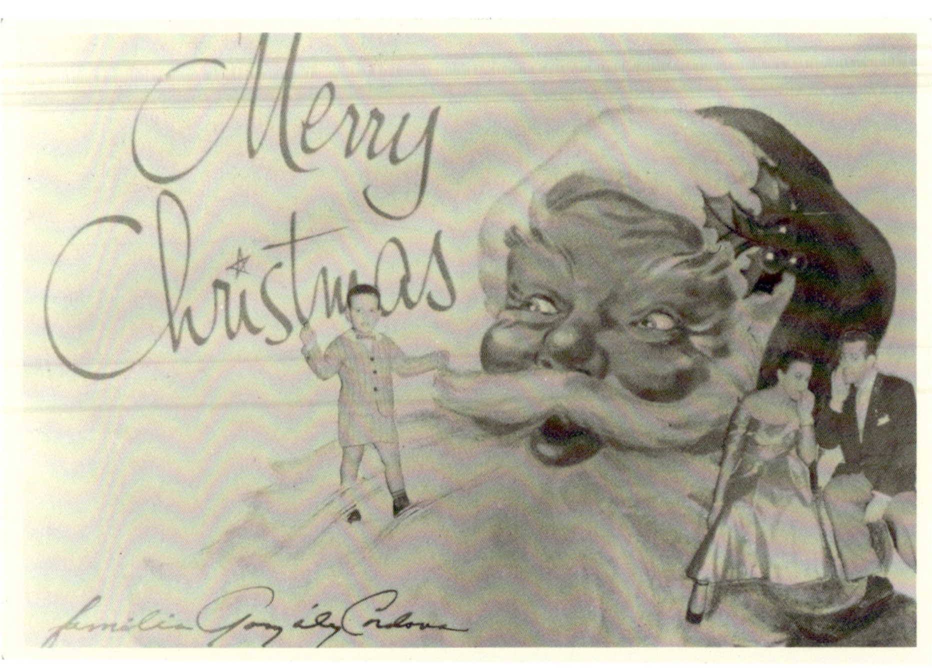
Merry Christmas
familia González Córdova

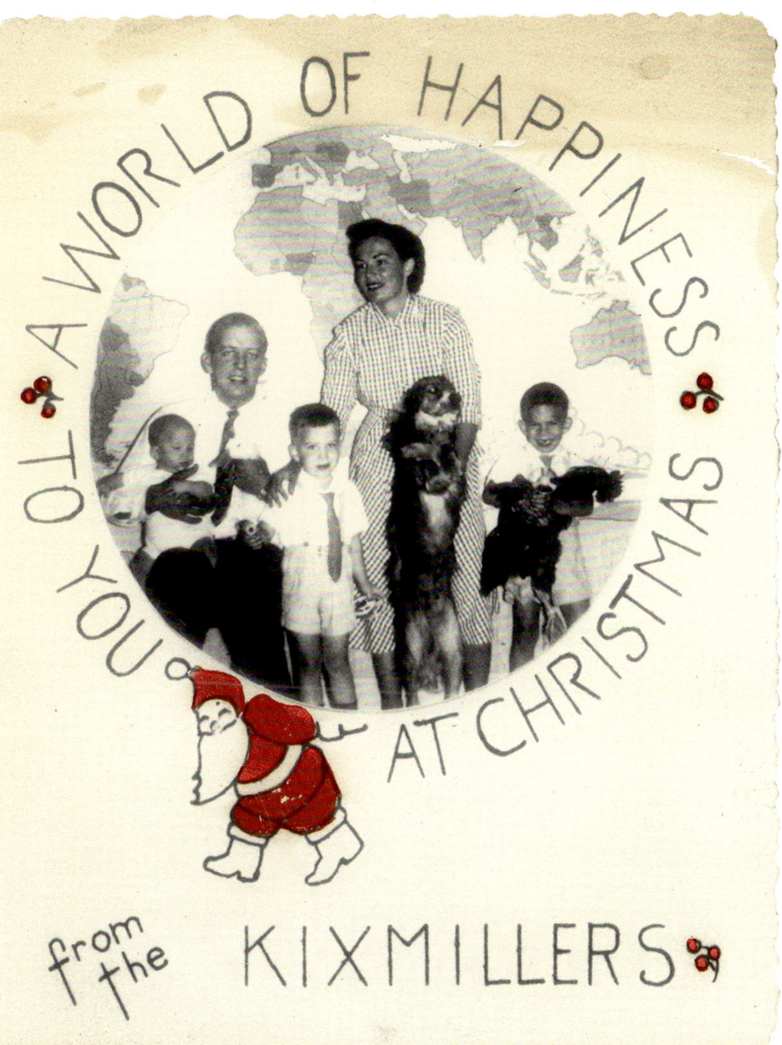

A WORLD OF HAPPINESS
TO YOU
AT CHRISTMAS
from the KIXMILLERS

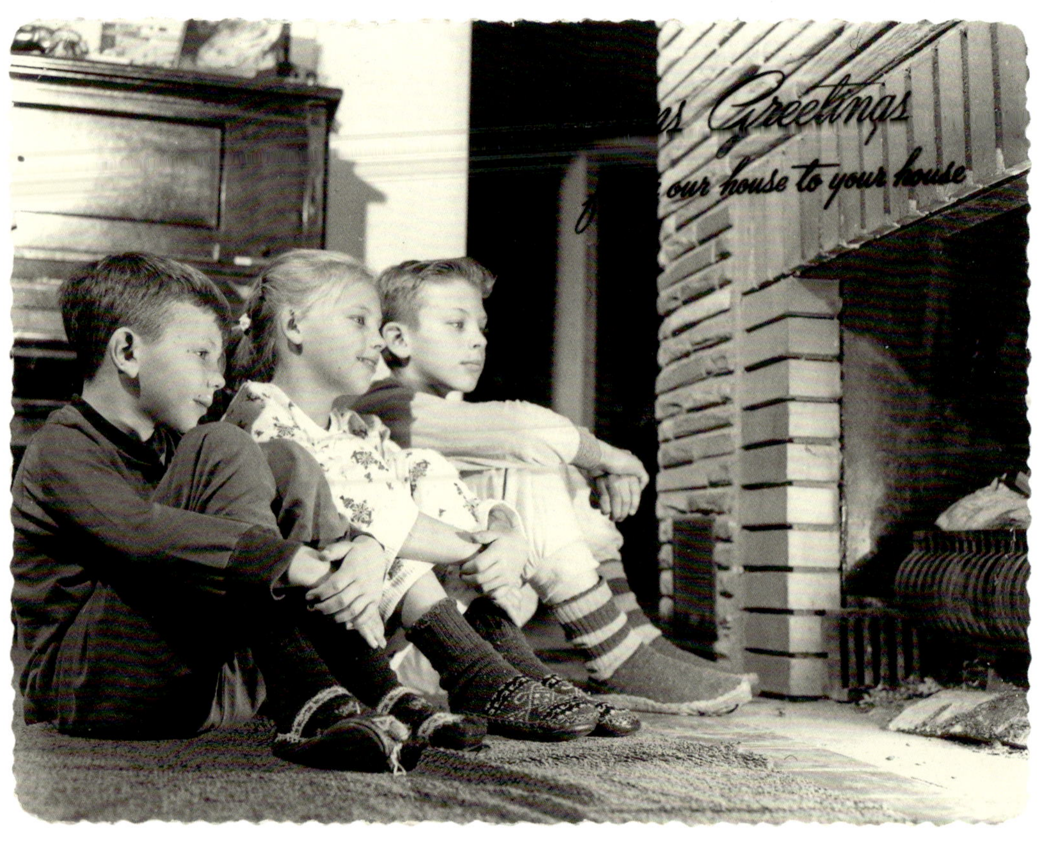

as Greetings
our house to your house

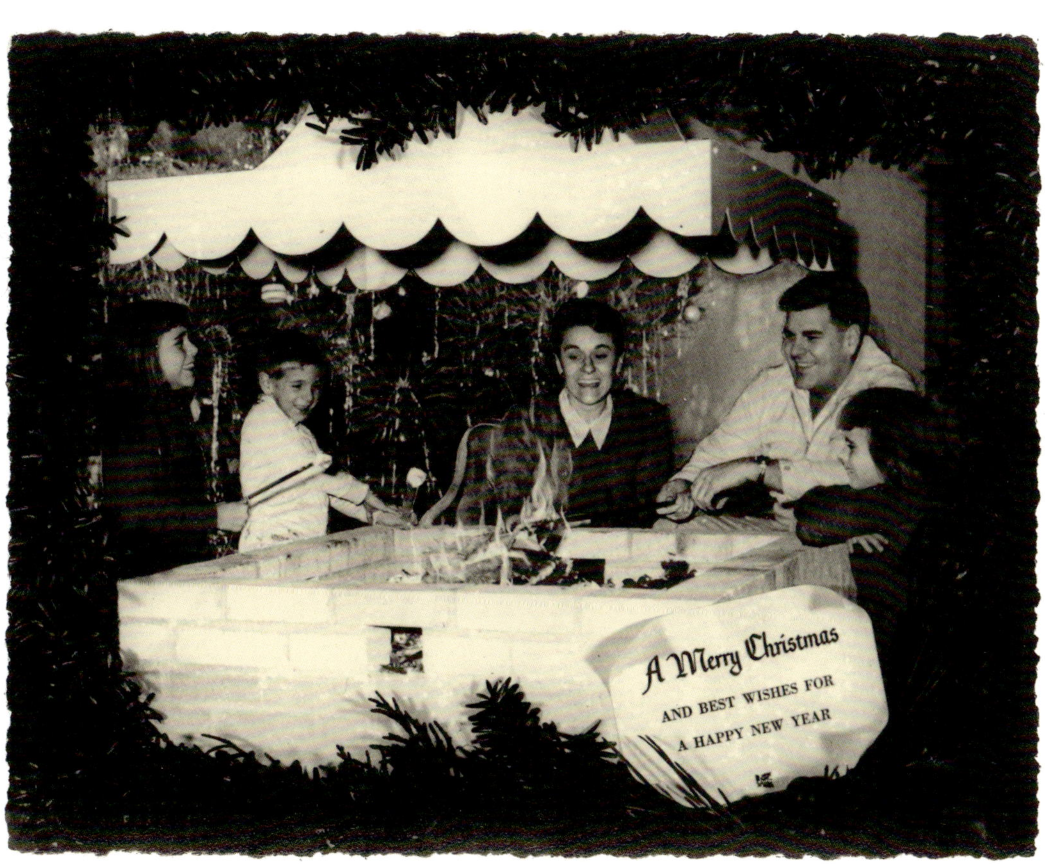
A Merry Christmas
AND BEST WISHES FOR
A HAPPY NEW YEAR

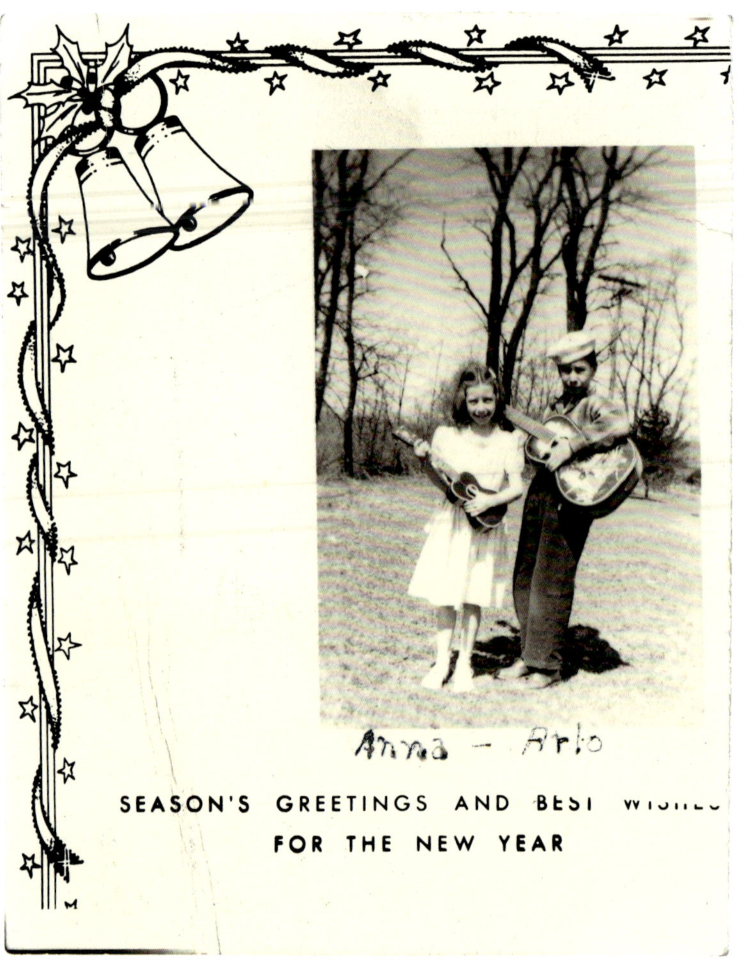

SEASON'S GREETINGS AND BEST WISHES
FOR THE NEW YEAR

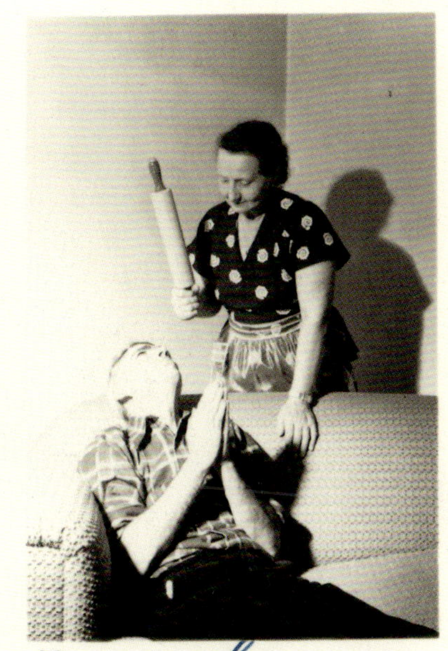

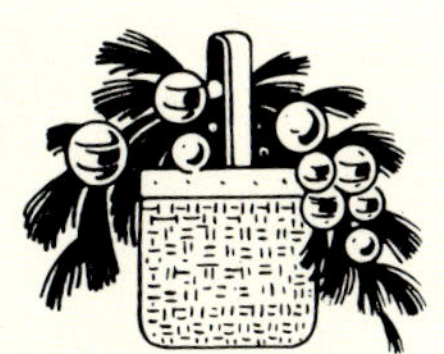

Best Wishes for a Very
Merry Christmas and
a Happy New Year...
☆

Frank & Walfred

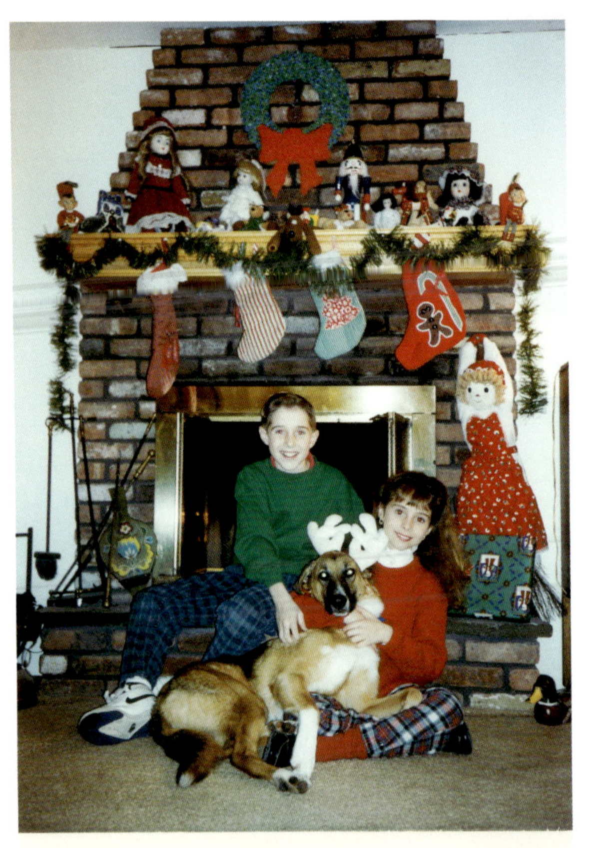

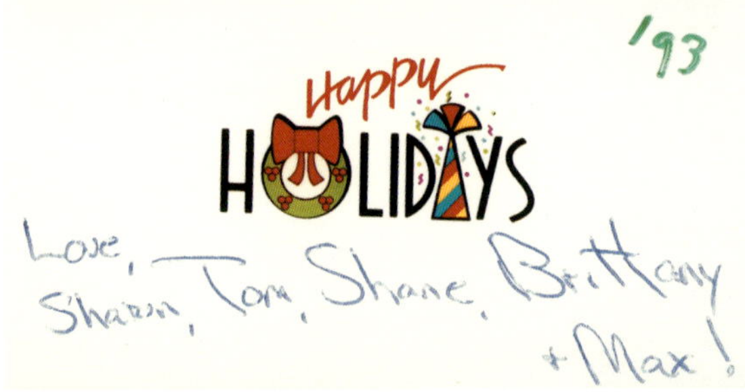

'93

Love,
Shawn, Tom, Shane, Brittany
& Max!

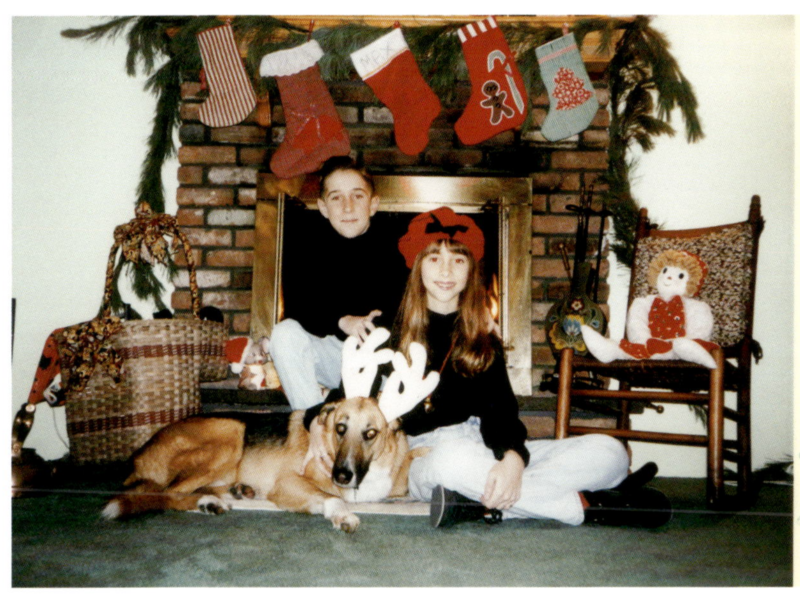

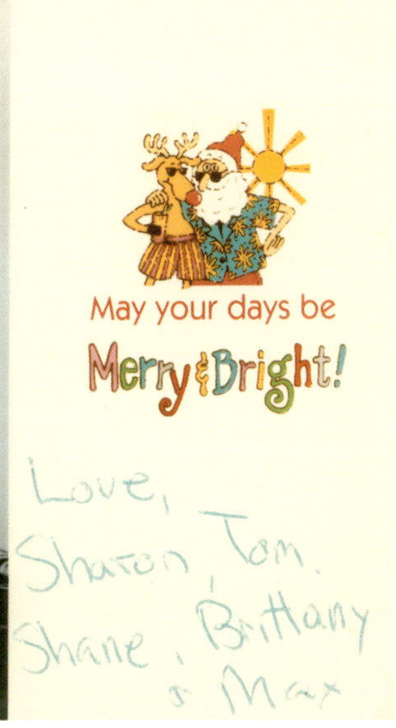

May your days be
Merry & Bright!
Love,
Sharon, Tom,
Shane, Brittany
& Max

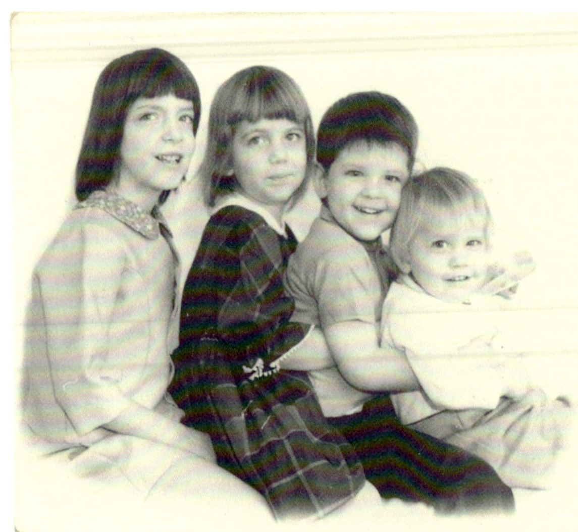

Season's Greetings

Dick + Merrilyn
Debbie, Deanna
Dick, Danny

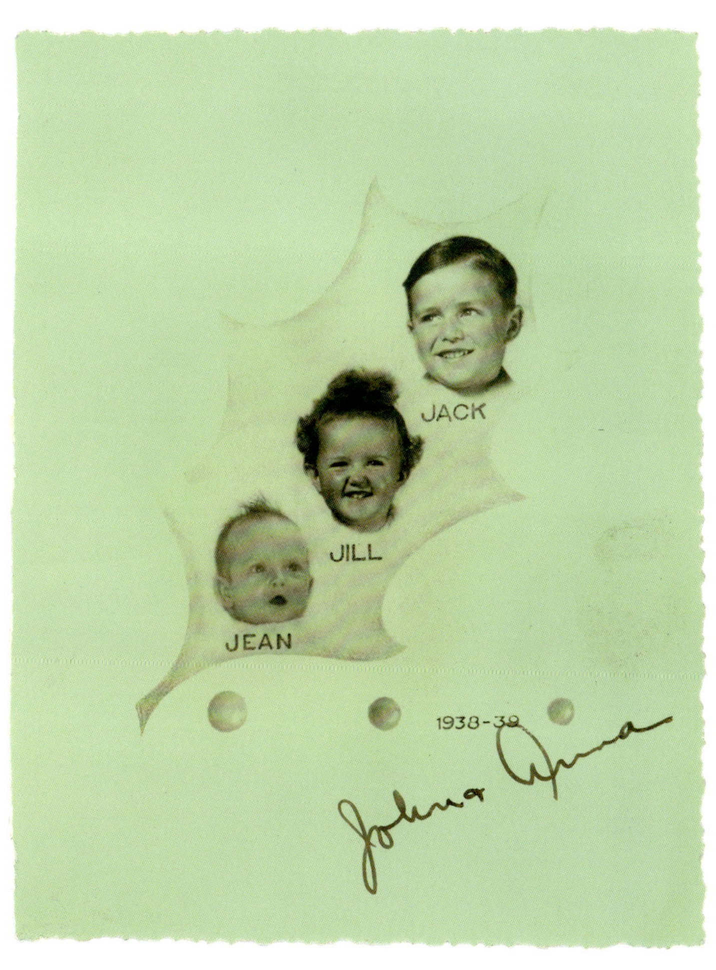

JACK
JILL
JEAN
1938-39

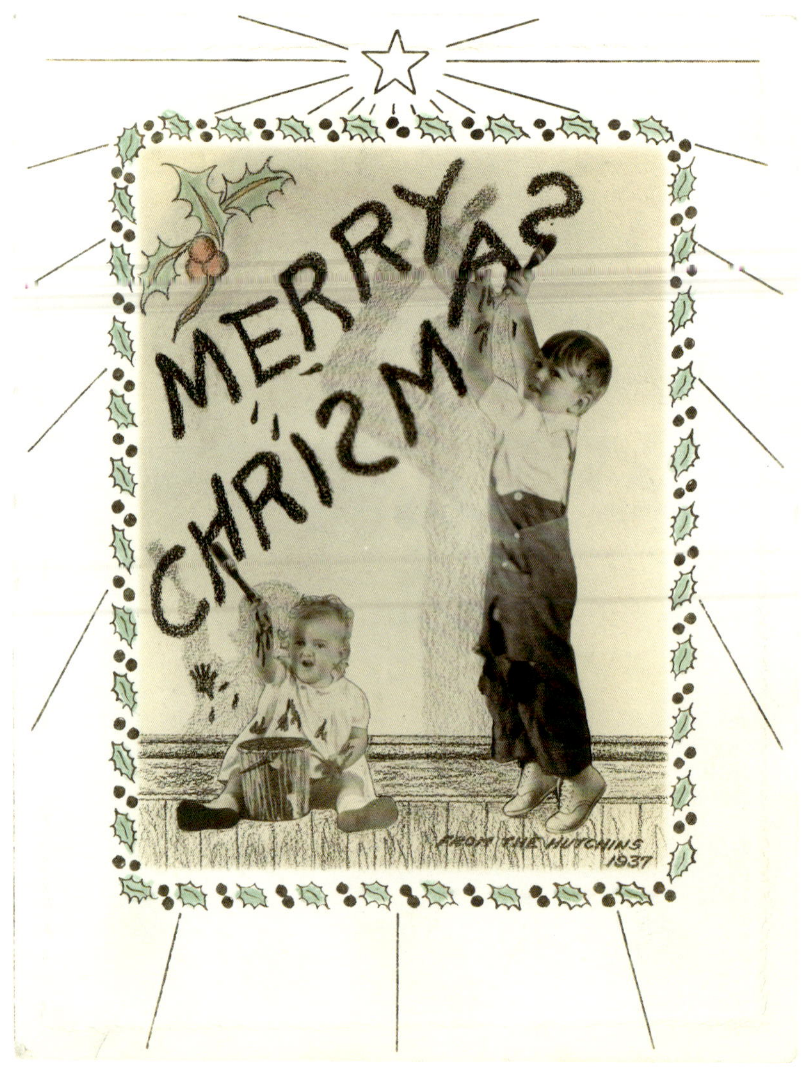

MERRY AS
CHRI2MS
FROM THE HUTCHINS
1937

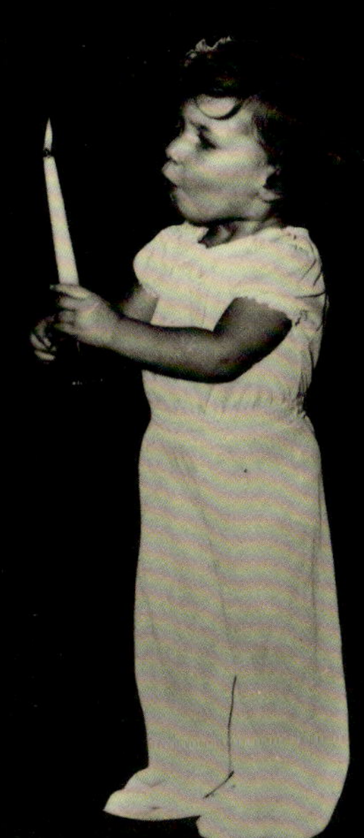

THE WITTS
SEASONS
GREETINGS

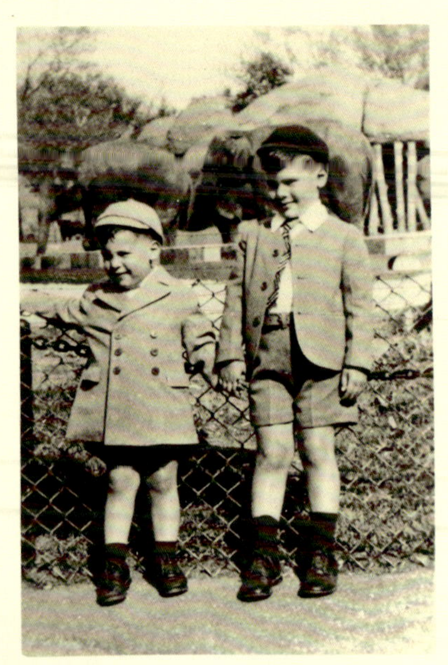

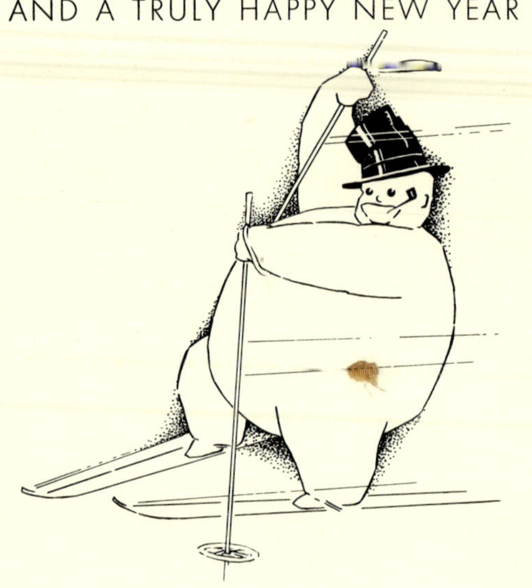

Major and Mrs. Joseph E. Barmack

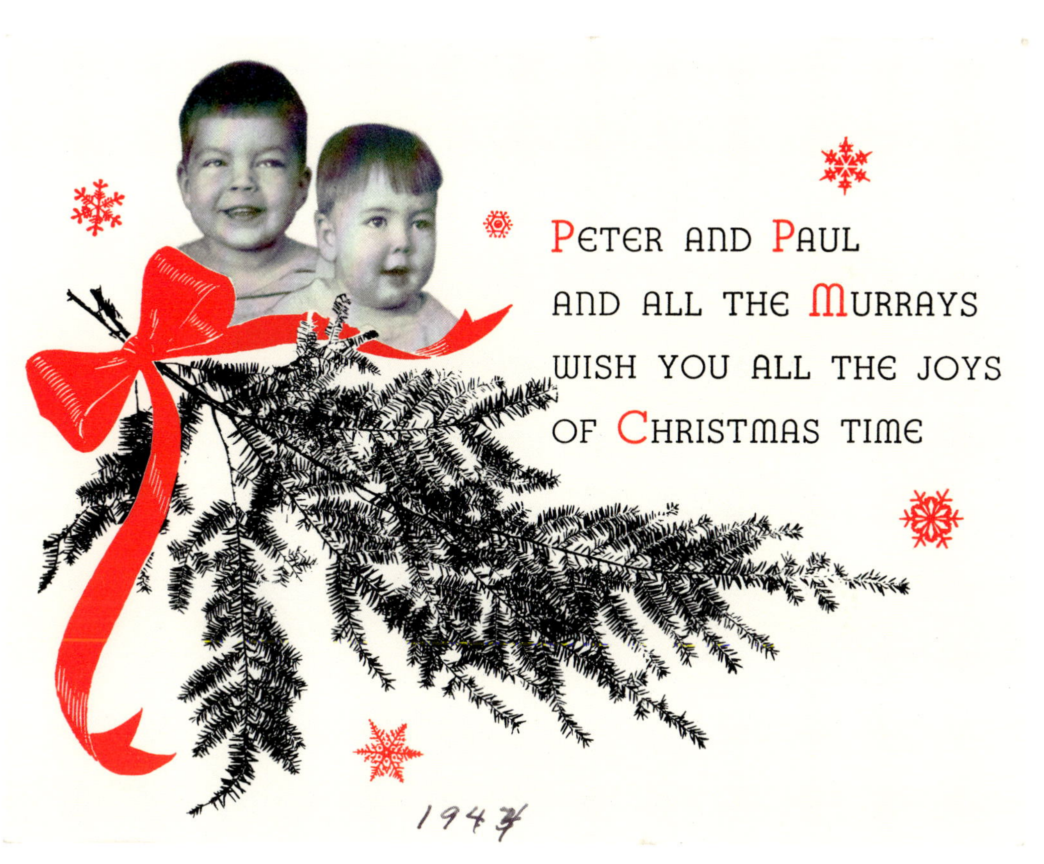
PETER AND PAUL
AND ALL THE MURRAYS
WISH YOU ALL THE JOYS
OF CHRISTMAS TIME
1947

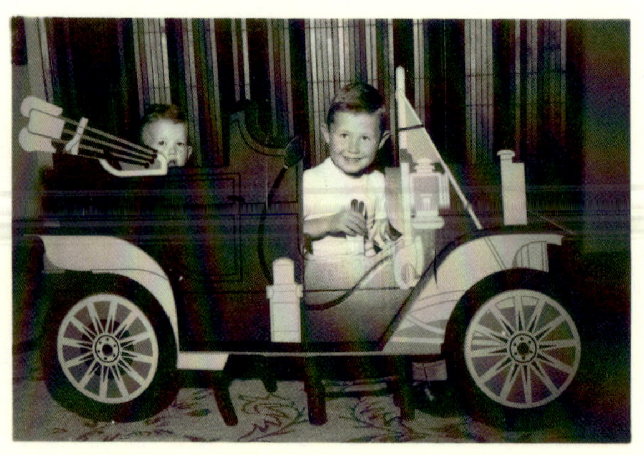

Season's Greetings

From::

Bobby, Jimmy, Jim & Shirley Holland

Meilleurs Vœux

pour

l'Année Nouvelle.

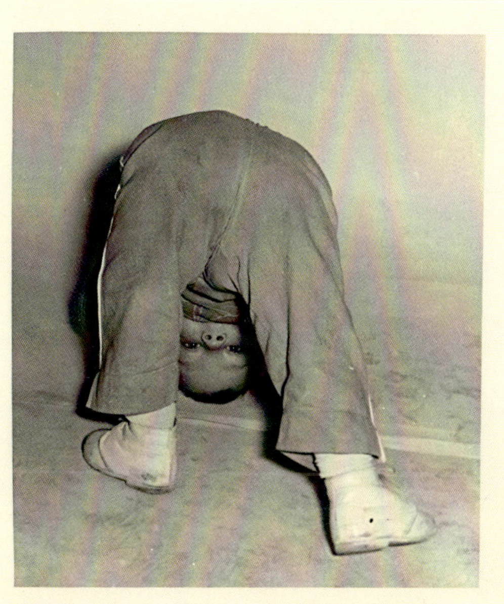

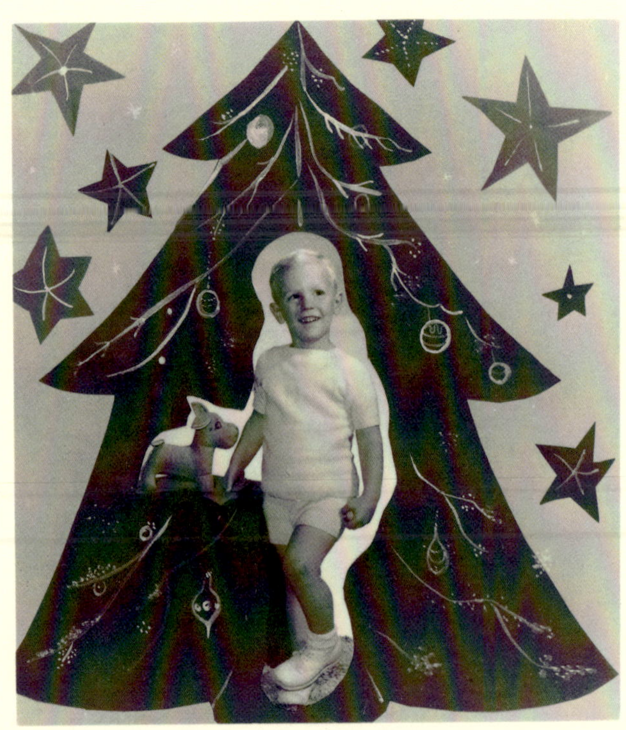

Merry Christmas and
a Happy New Year...

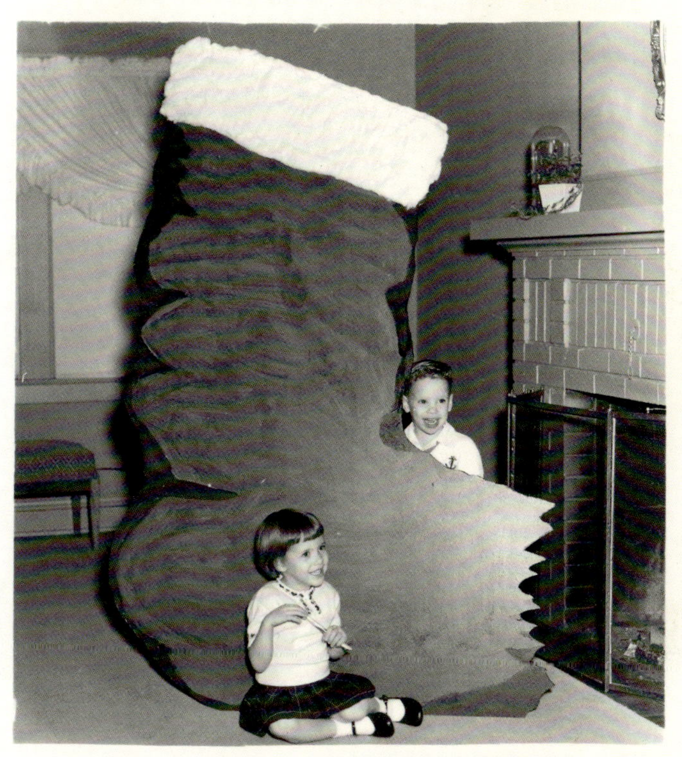

Season's Greetings

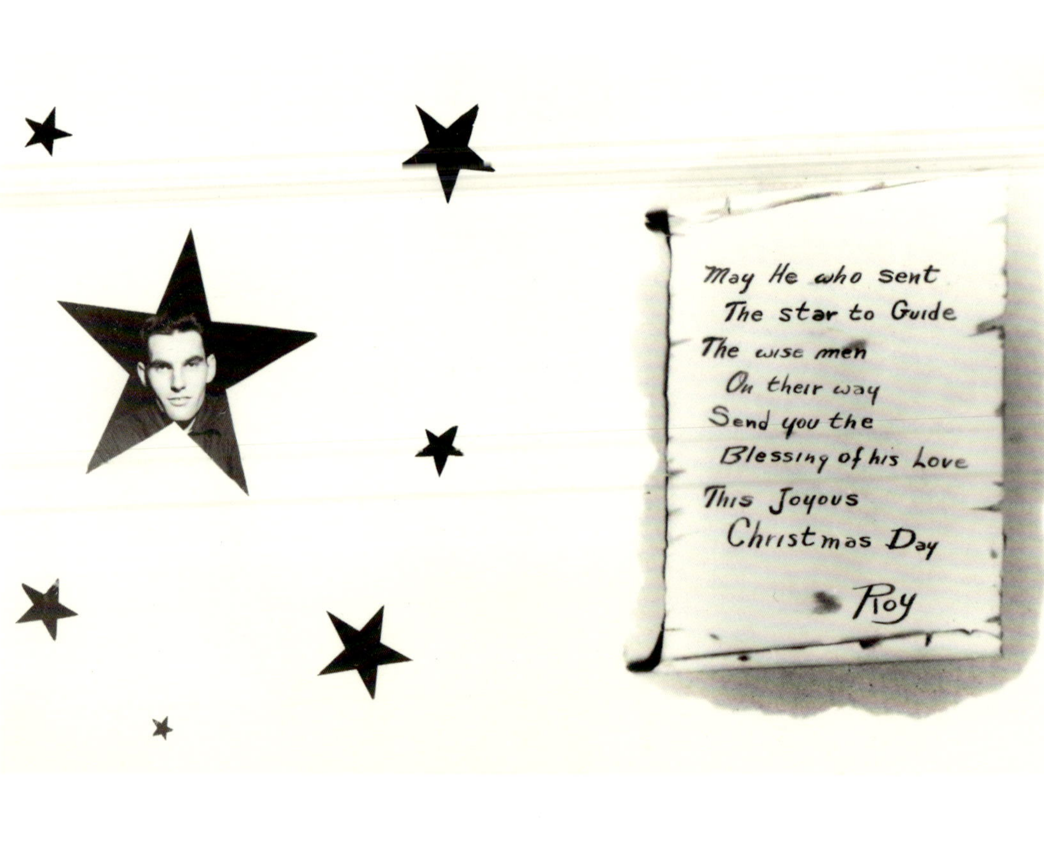

May He who sent
The star to Guide
The wise men
On their way
Send you the
Blessing of his Love
This Joyous
Christmas Day

Roy

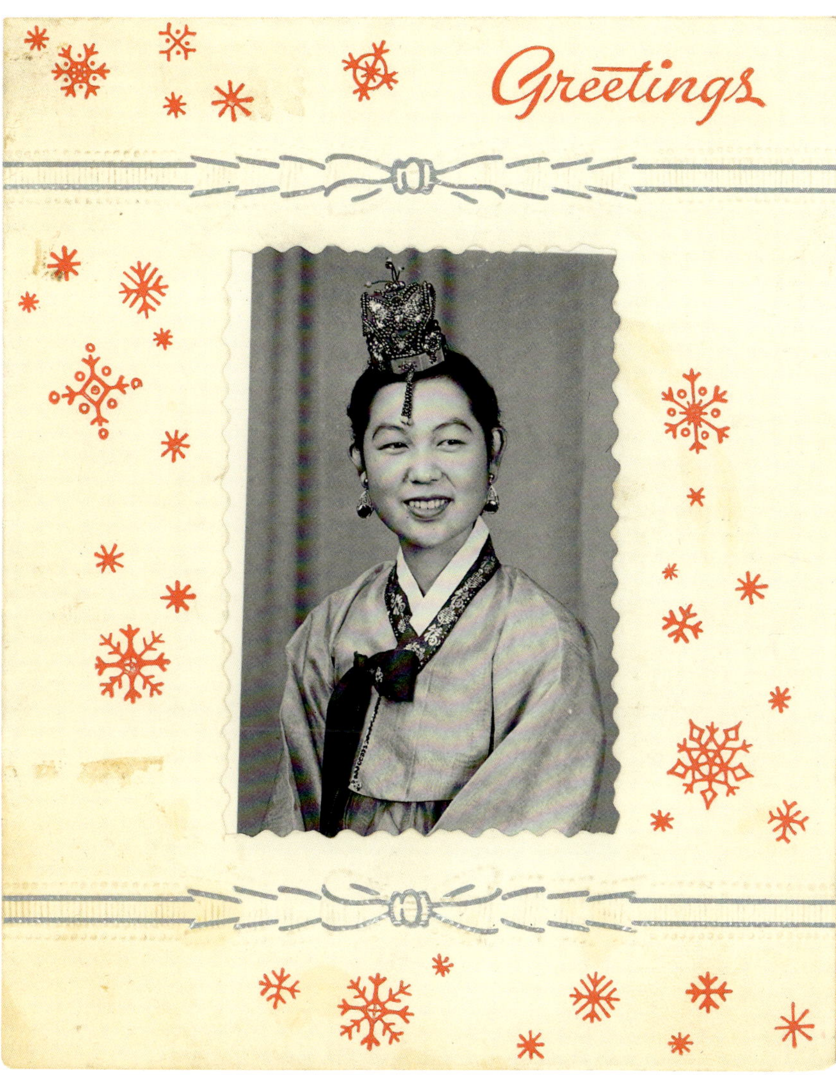

Greetings

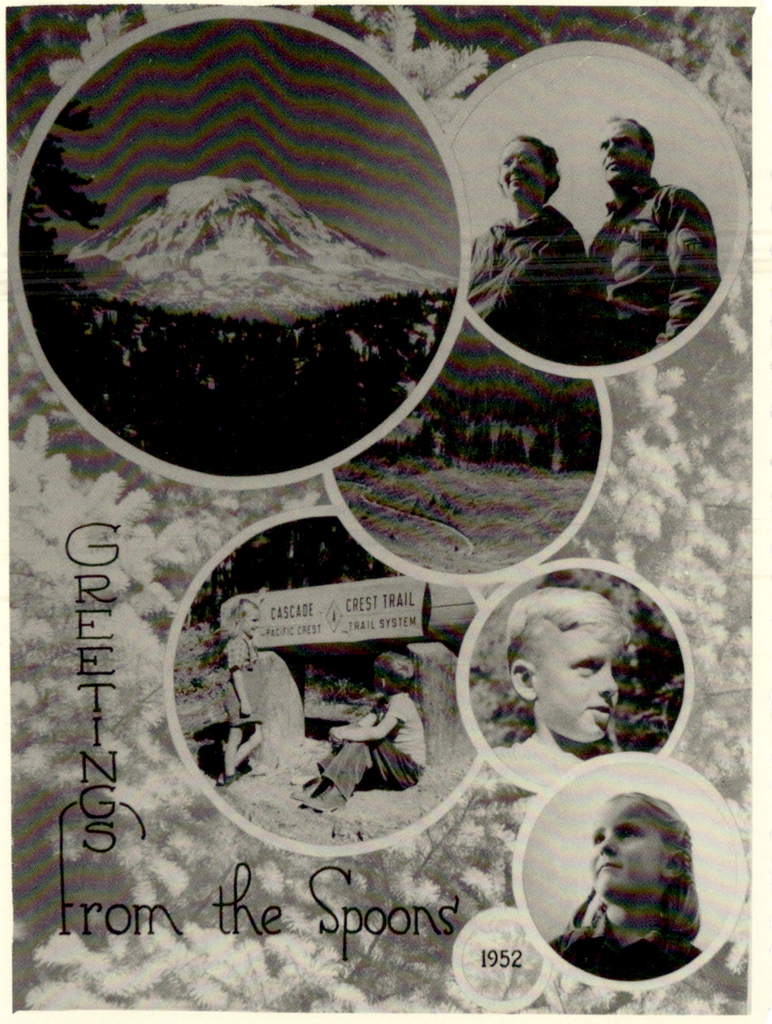
CASCADE
CREST TRAIL
PACIFIC CREST
TRAIL SYSTEM
GREETINGS
from the Spoons
1952

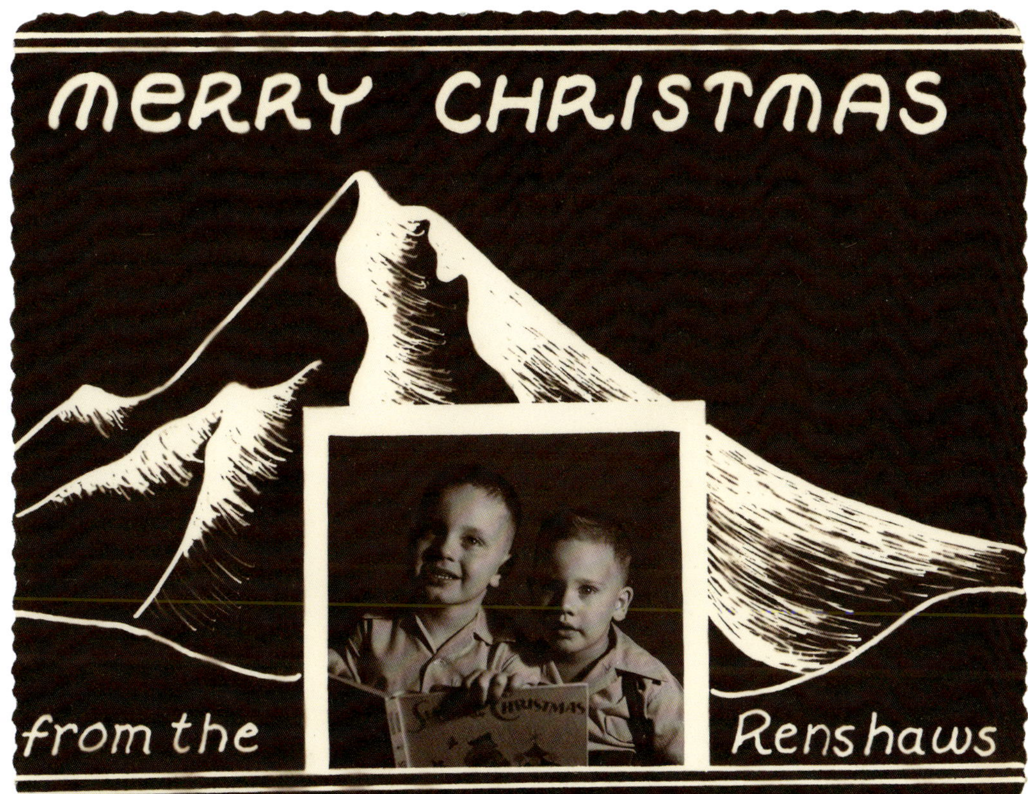

MERRY CHRISTMAS
from the
Renshaws

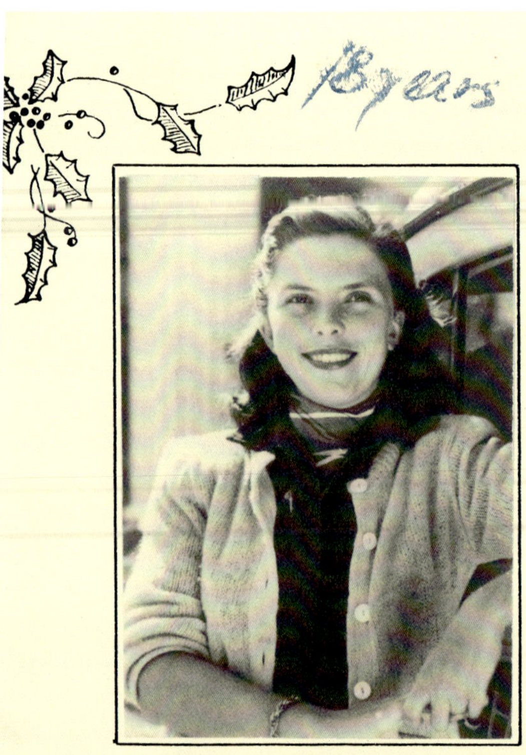

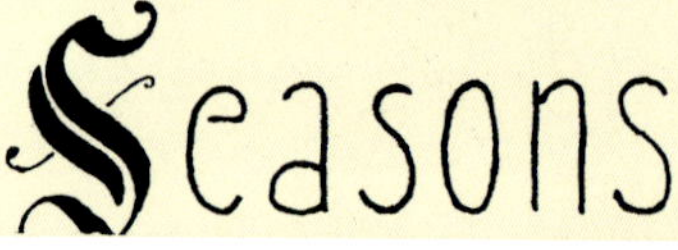

Seasons

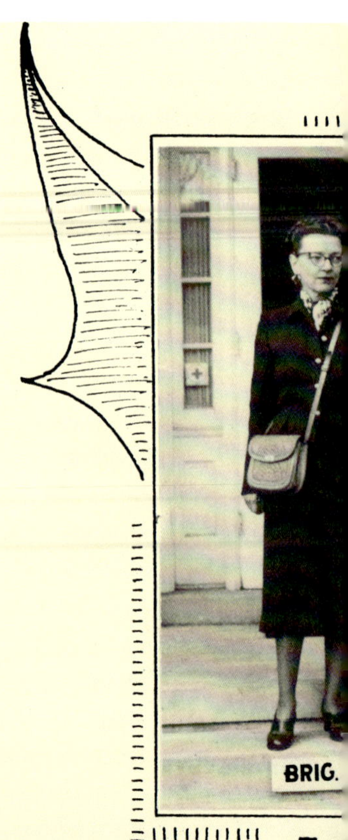

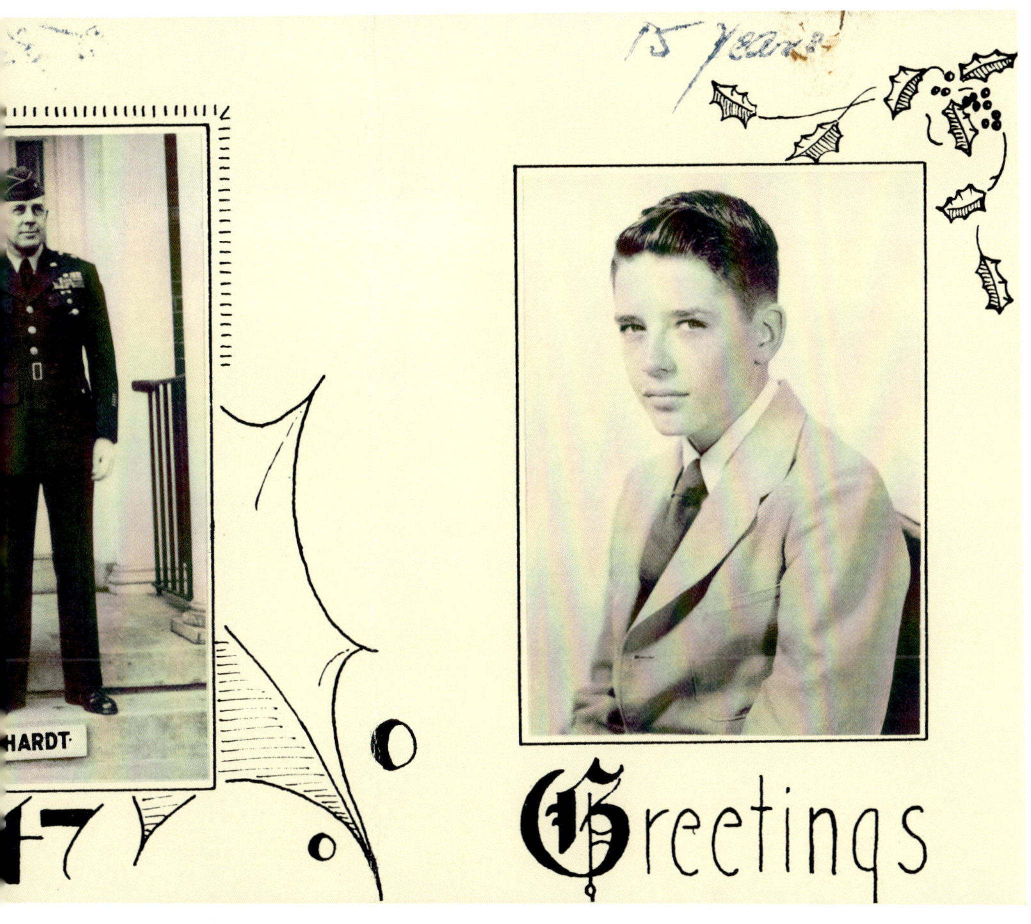
15 years
HARDT
47
Greetings

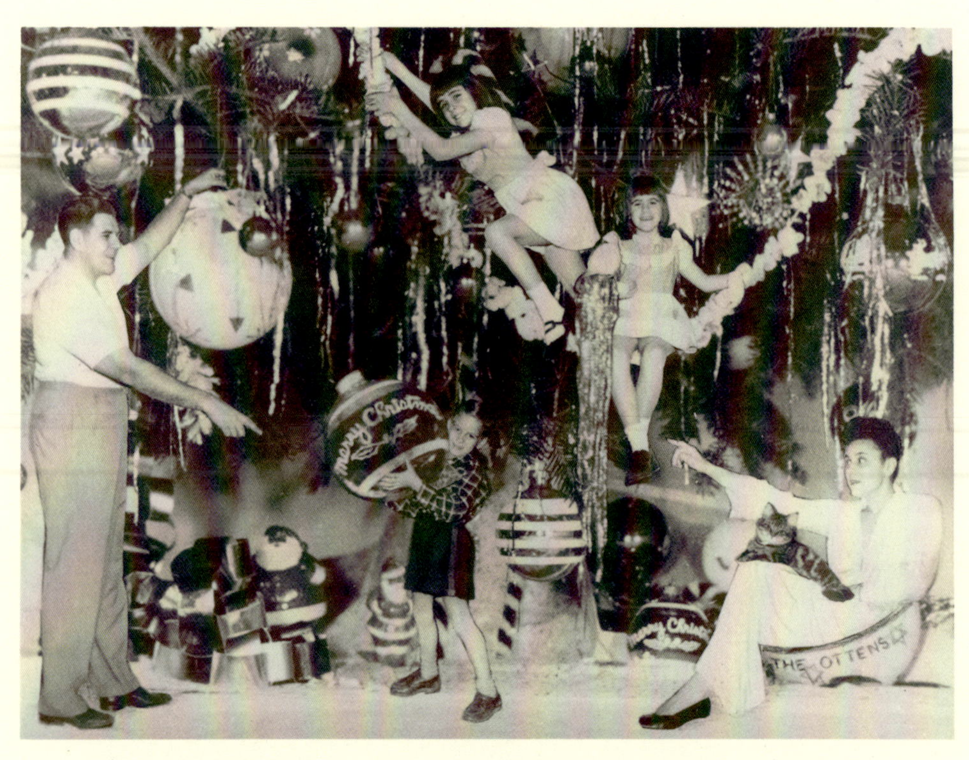
Merry Christmas
THE OTTENS

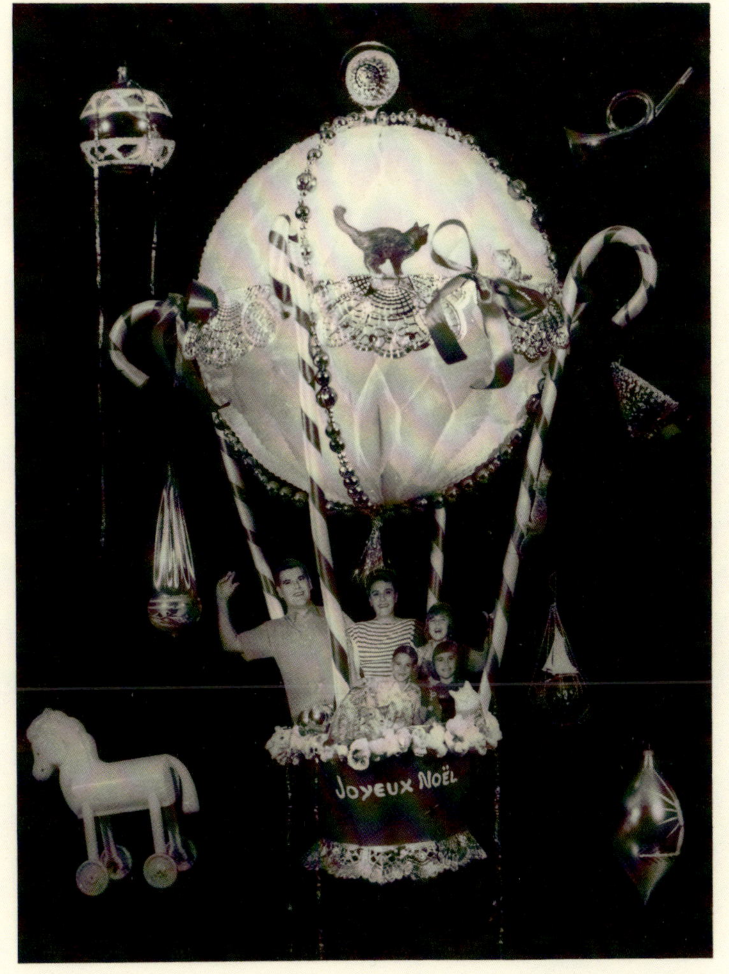

Joyeux Noël

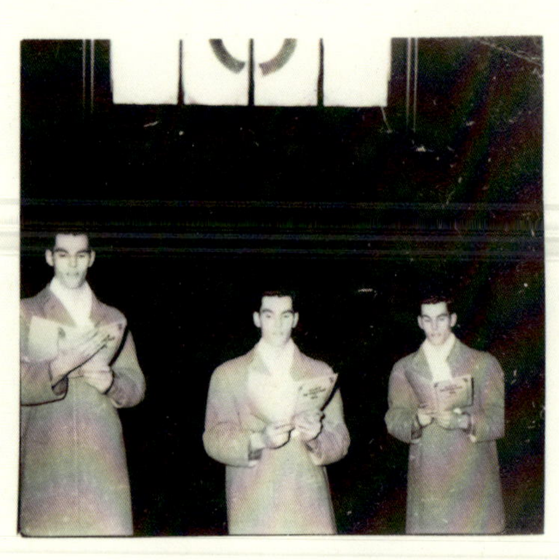

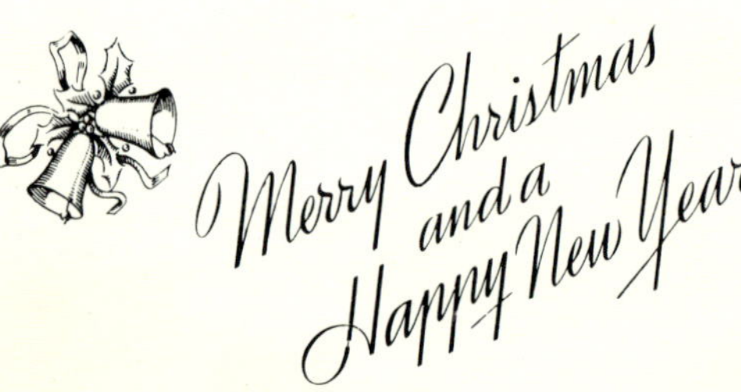
Merry Christmas
and a
Happy New Year

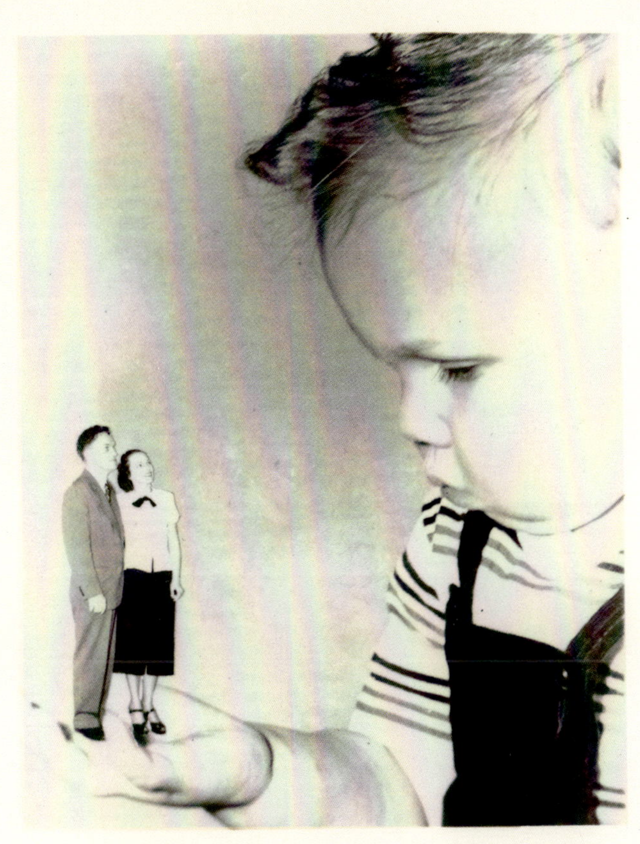

A Merry Christmas

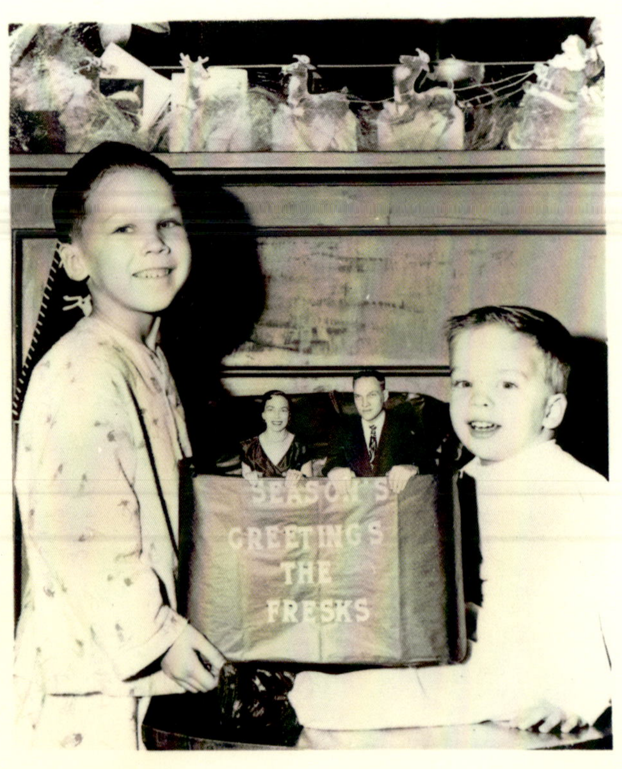
SEASON'S
GREETINGS
THE
FRESKS

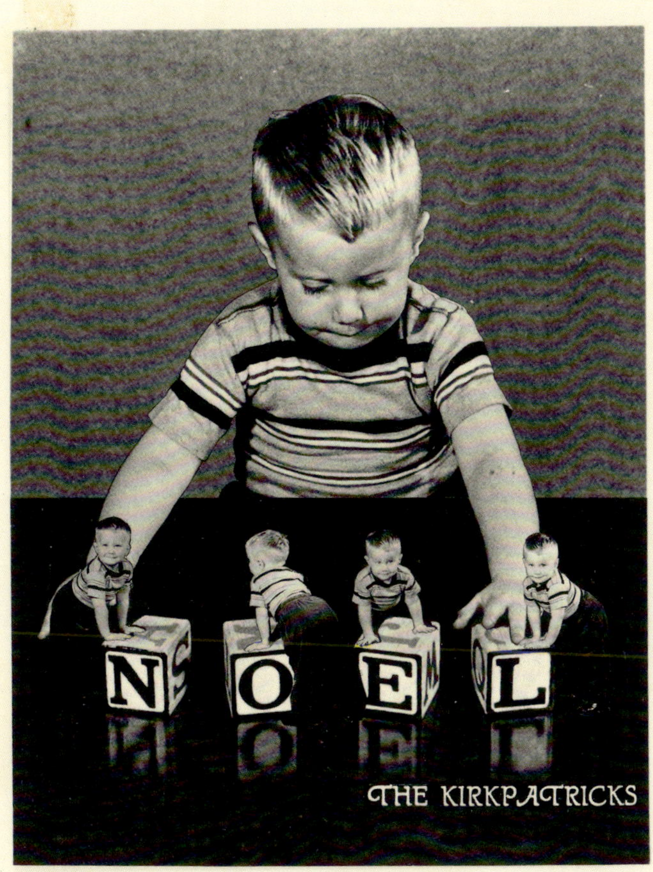

NOEL
THE KIRKPATRICKS

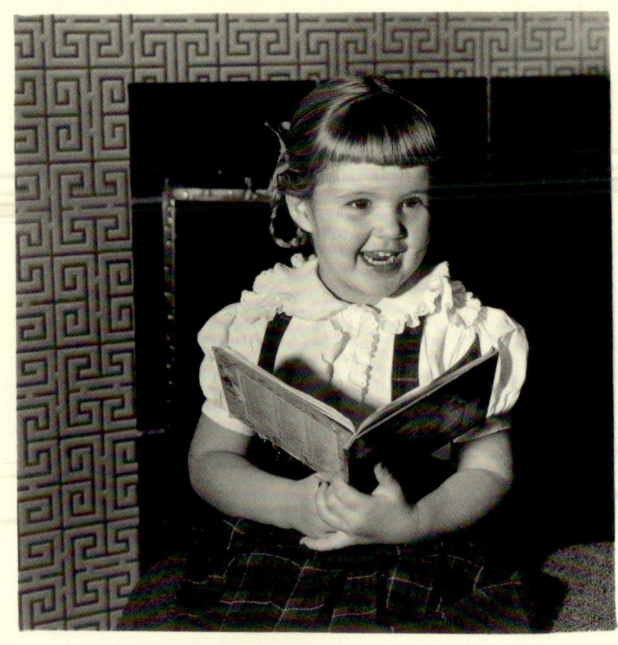

merry
christmas!

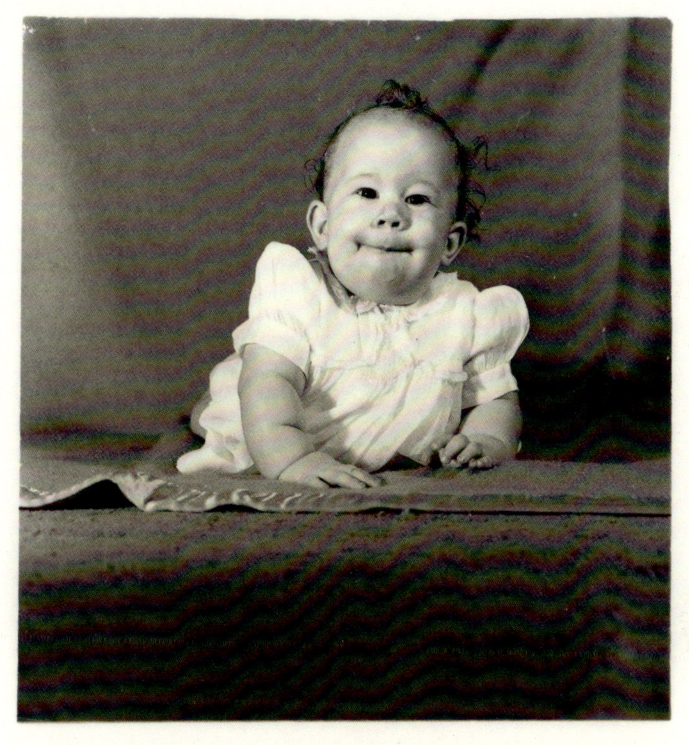

Season's Greetings

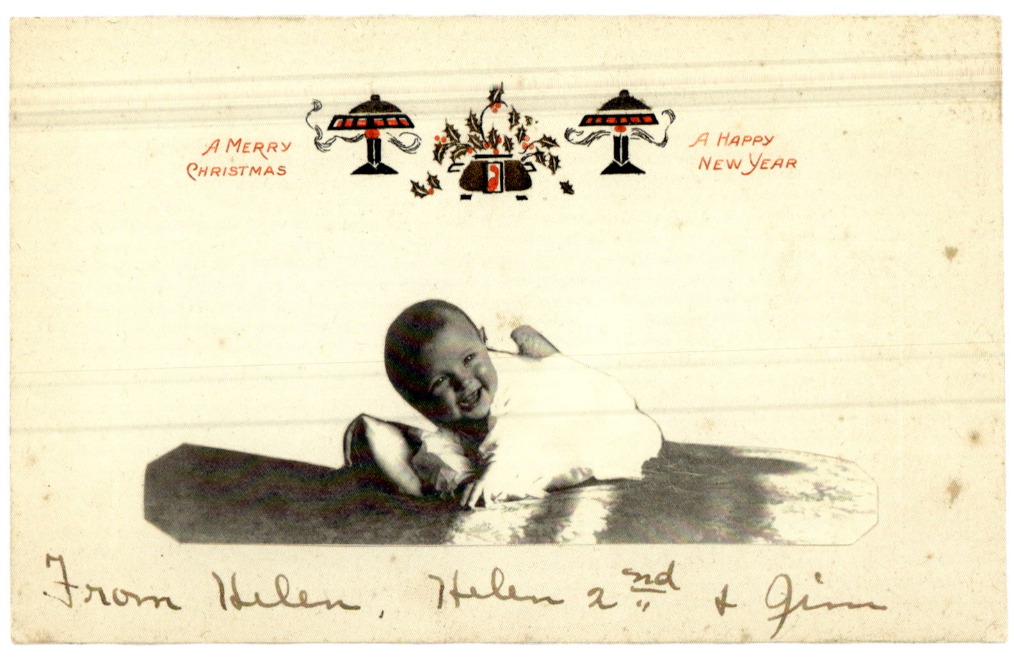

From Helen, Helen 2nd & Jim

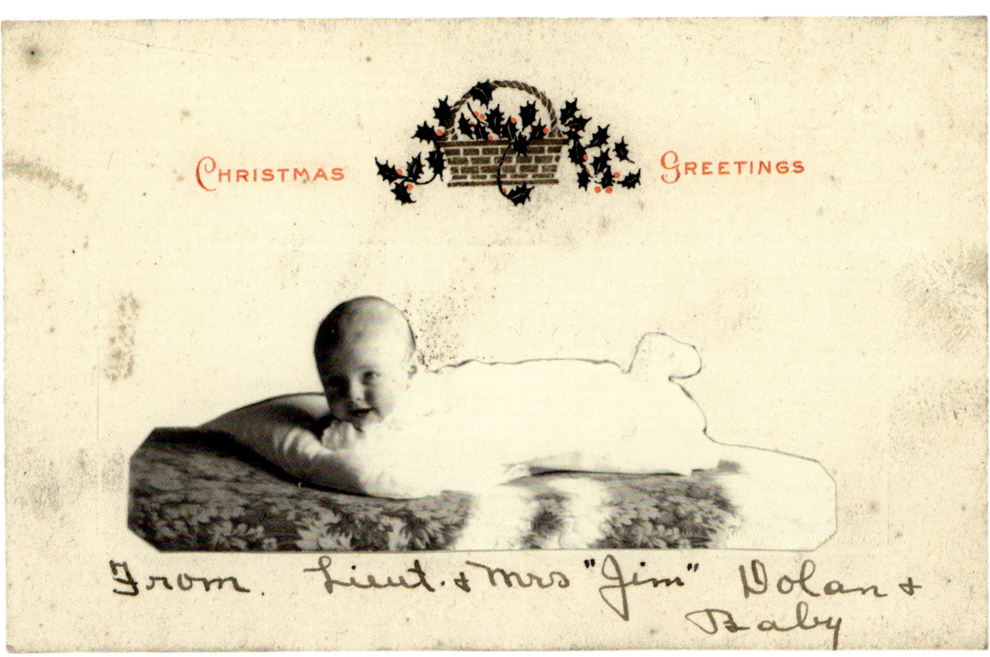

CHRISTMAS
GREETINGS
From Lieut. & Mrs "Jim" Dolan & Baby

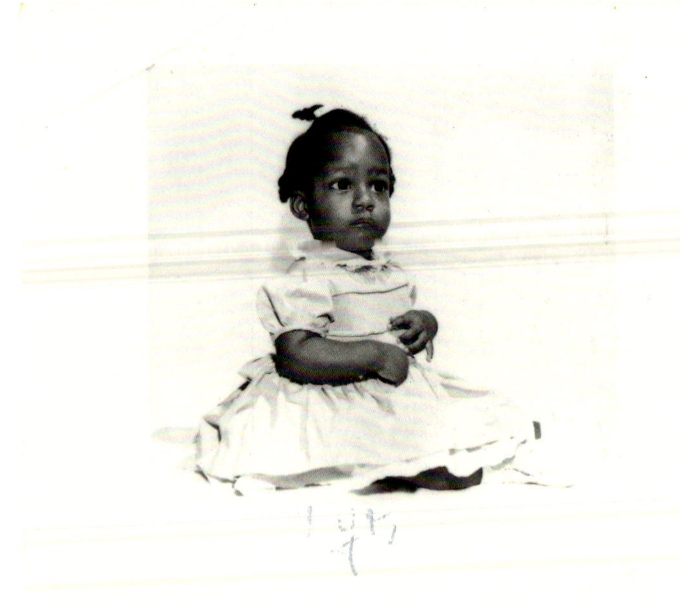

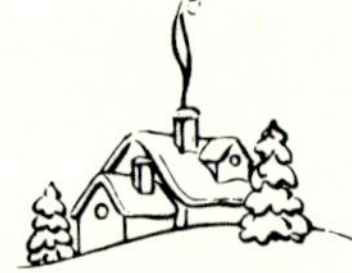

Season's
GREETINGS

FROM OUR HOUSE TO YOUR HOUSE

love

Vernon, Sonk Lind

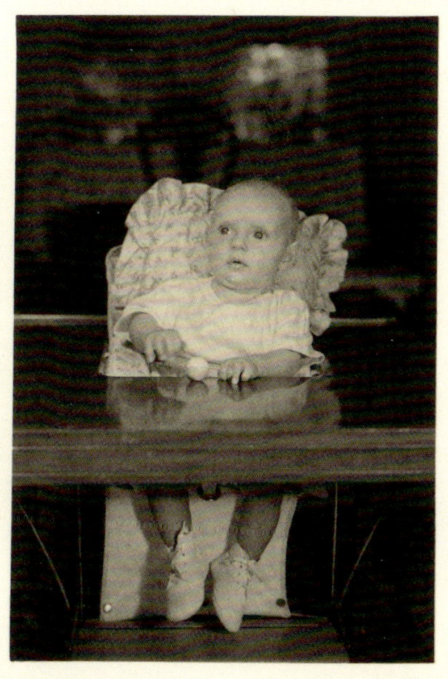

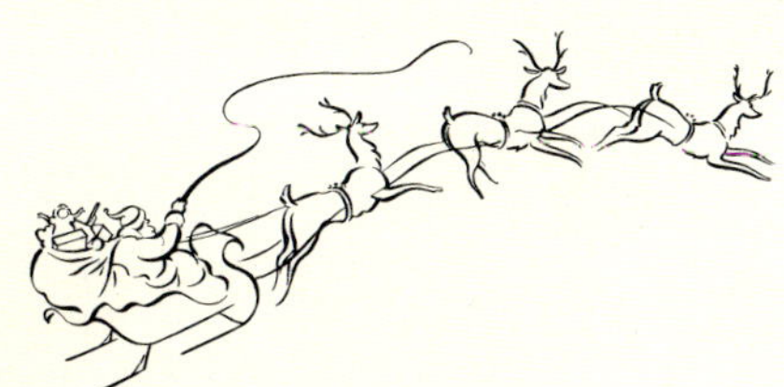

Merry
Christmas

Walter, Ellen & Vincent

Season's Greetings

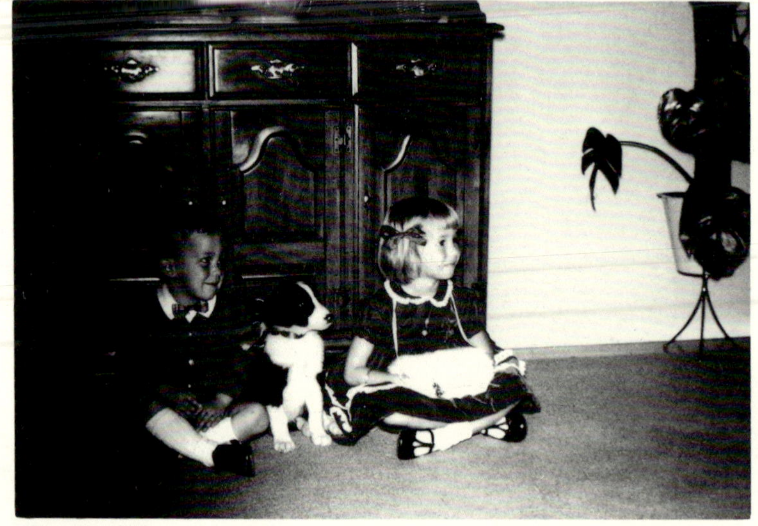

Love,
The Ken Coover Family

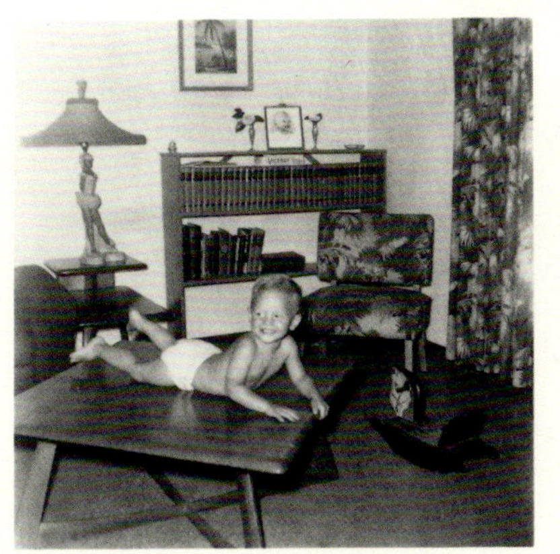

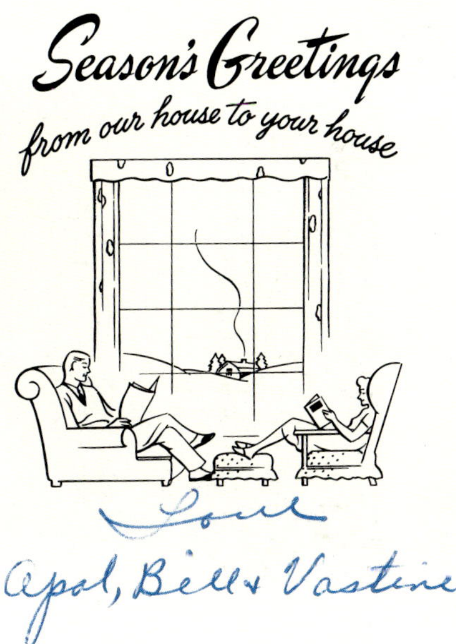

Love
Apol, Bill & Vastine

(over)

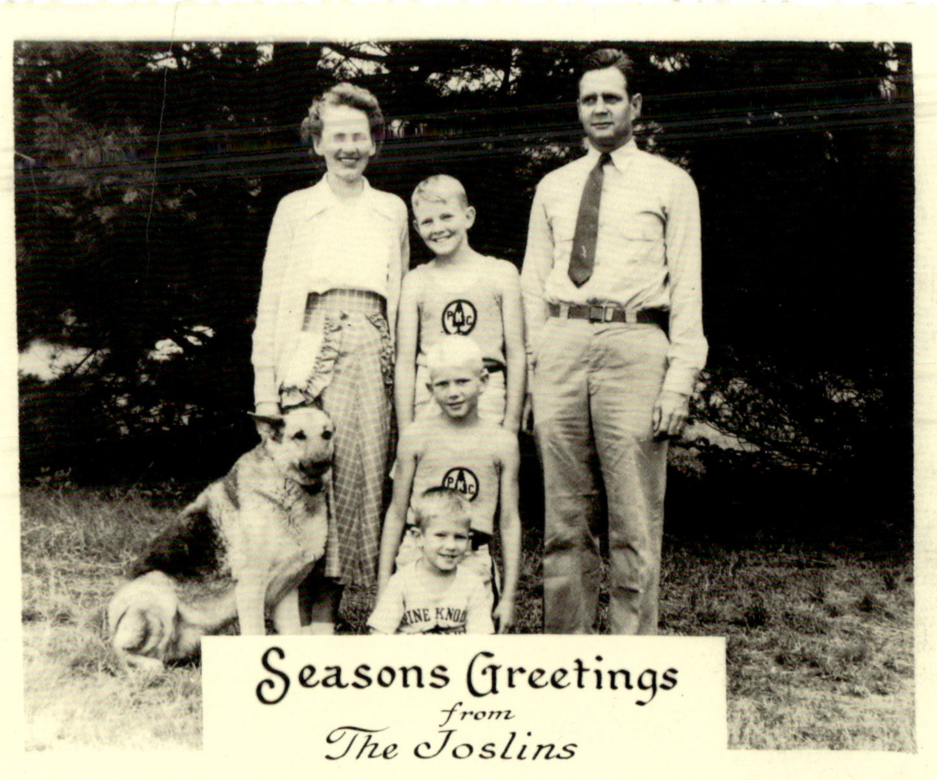

Seasons Greetings
from
The Joslins

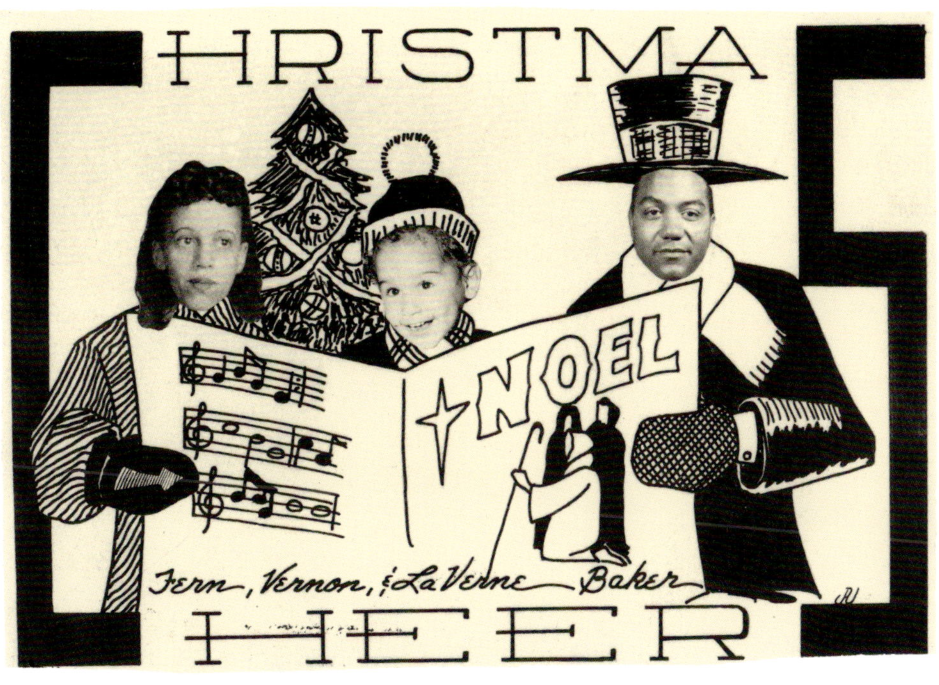

CHRISTMAS
NOEL
Fern, Vernon, & LaVerne   Baker
CHEER

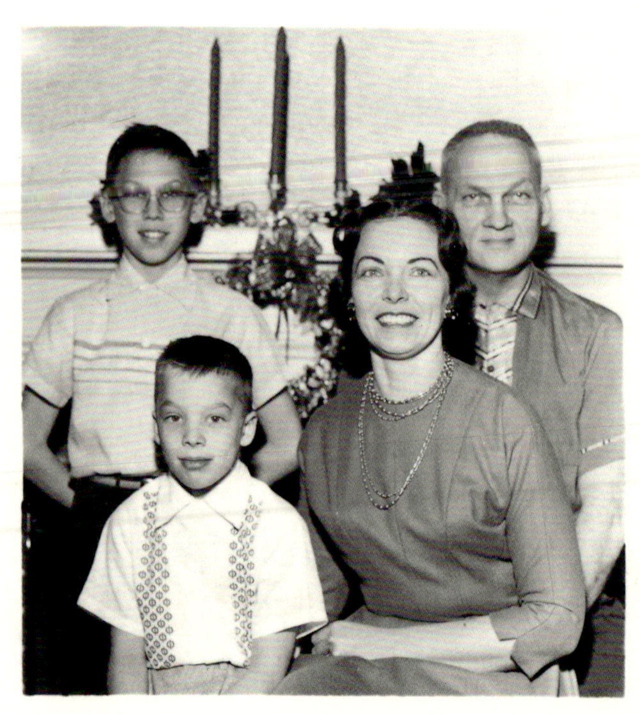

A Merry Christmas

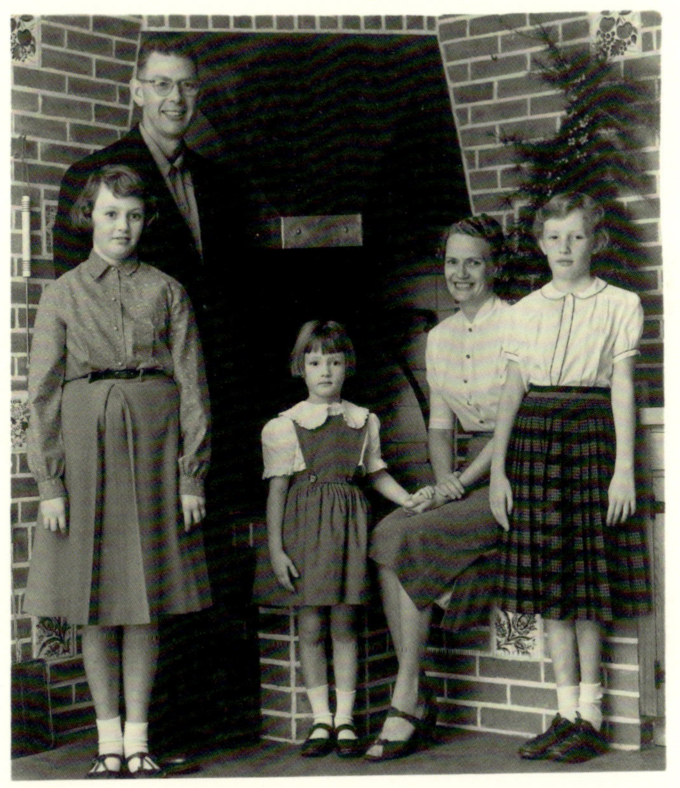

Season's Greetings

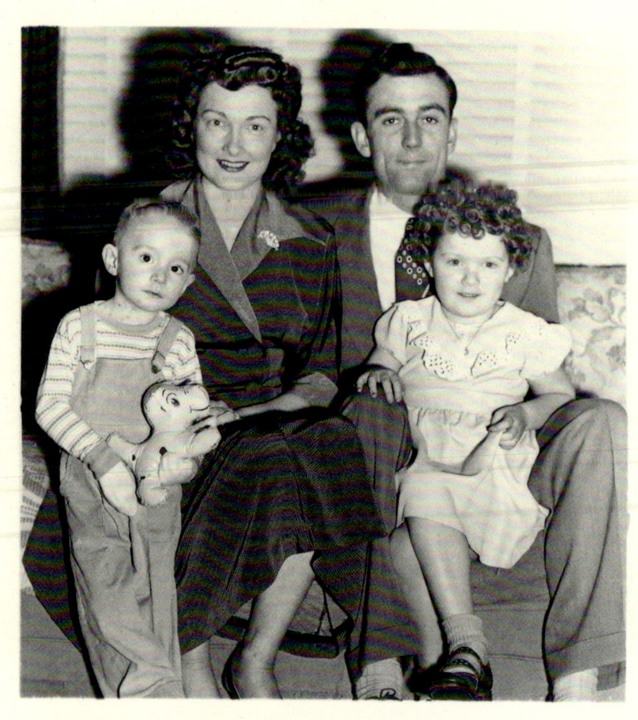

A Merry Christmas

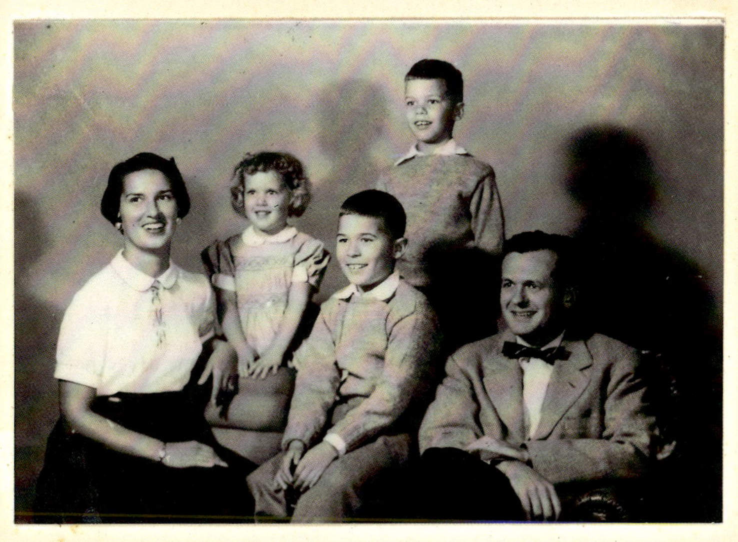

Once A Year The Pages Turn

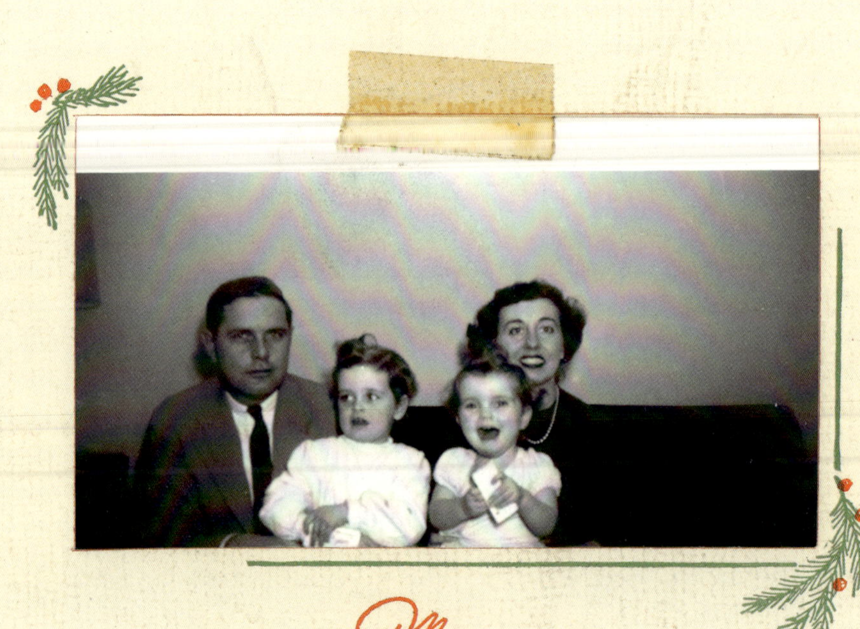

Merry
Christmas

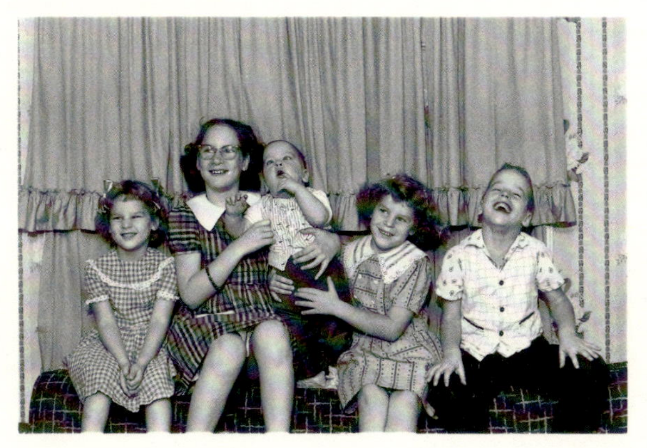

Merry Christmas
Happy New Year
The Remleys

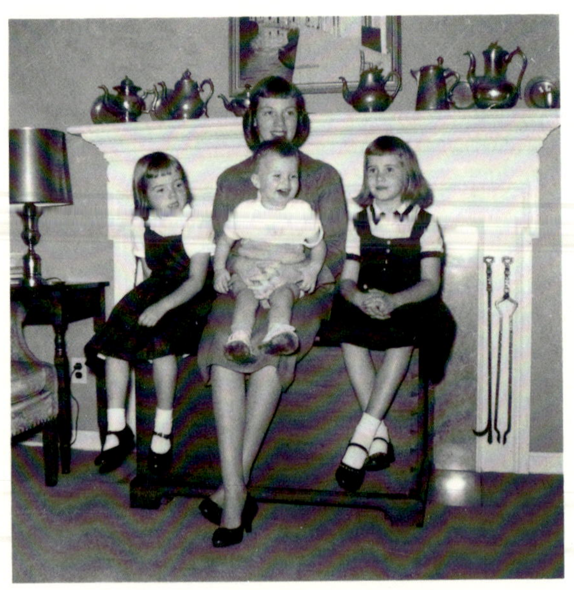

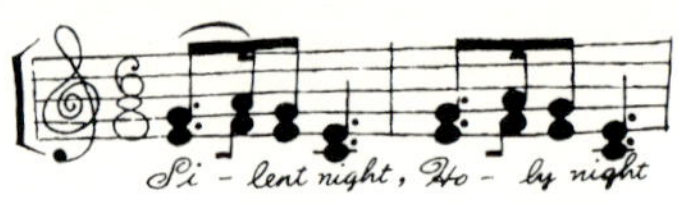

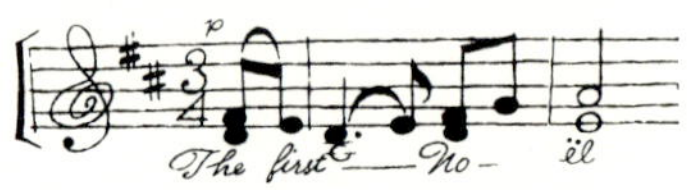

Mr. Coulianses

(over)

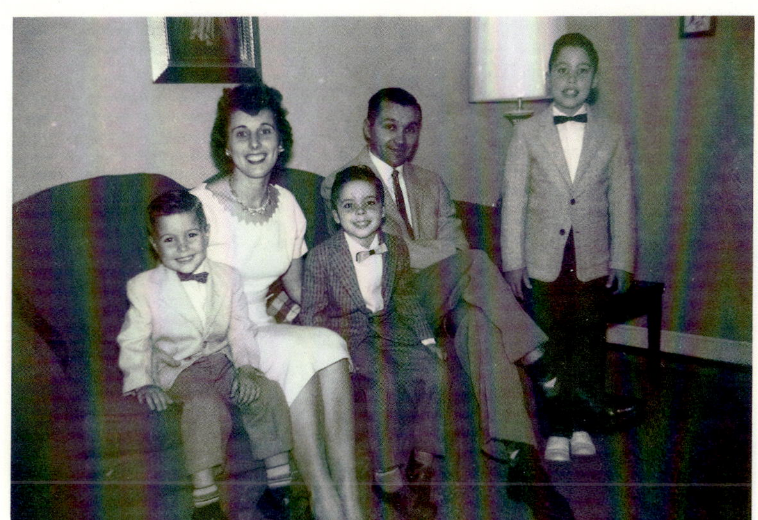

SEASON'S
GREETINGS
The Pocalyko family

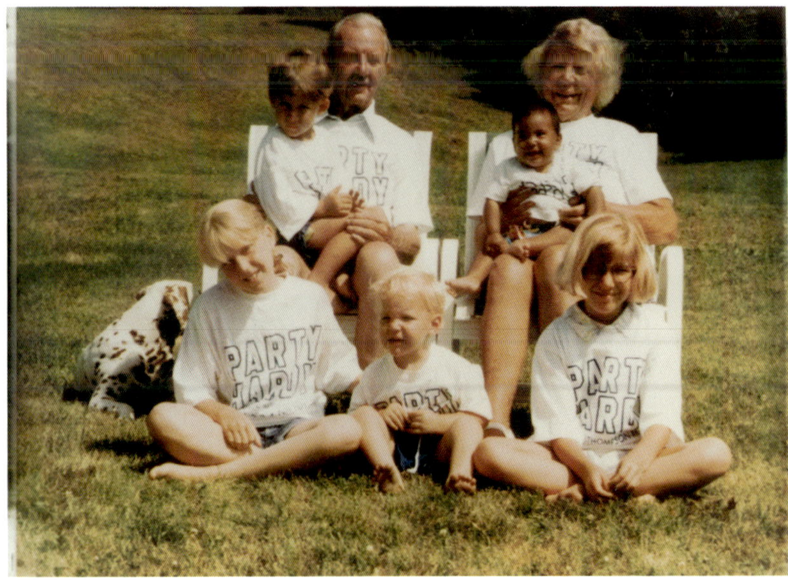

'93

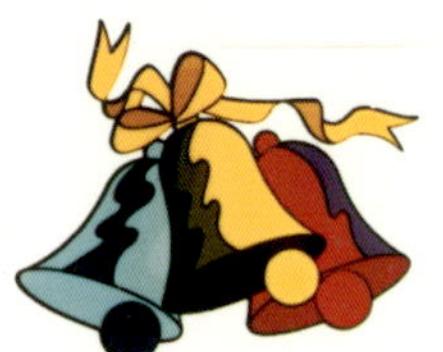

Victor   Esther
Will   Olivia
Heather, August, Danielle
          & Lil M Chips
July 6, 1993, N.H.

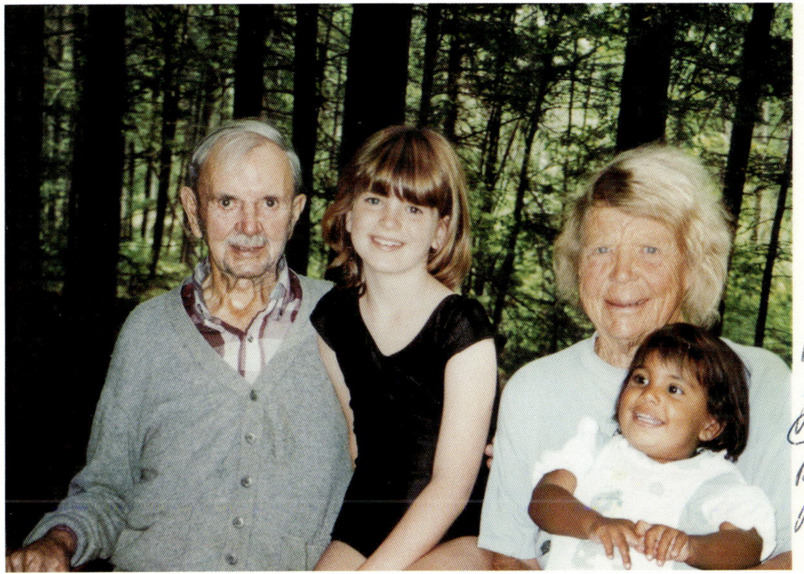

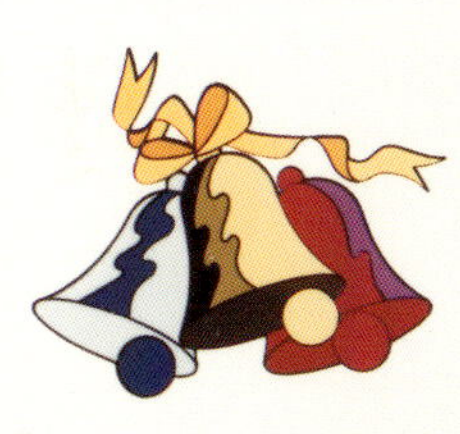

Victor Esther
grand daughters
Cassie Olivia
Belgrade Lakes
August 1994

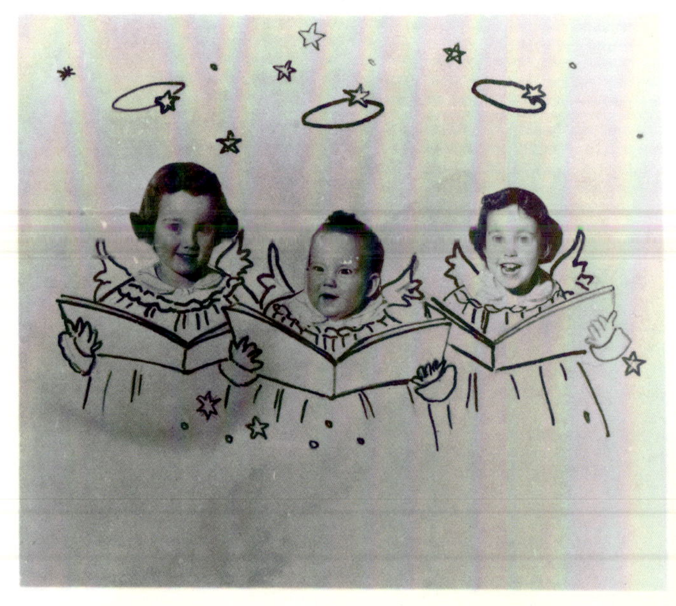

Season's Greetings

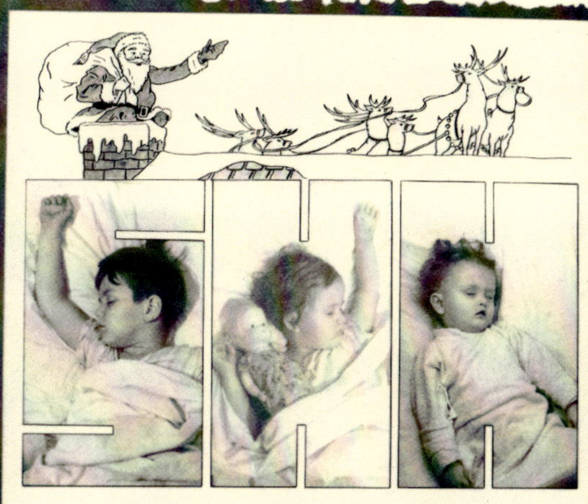

SANTA'S COMIN' AGAIN
AND
THE SEASONS GREETINGS
FROM THE HUTCHINS
1939-40

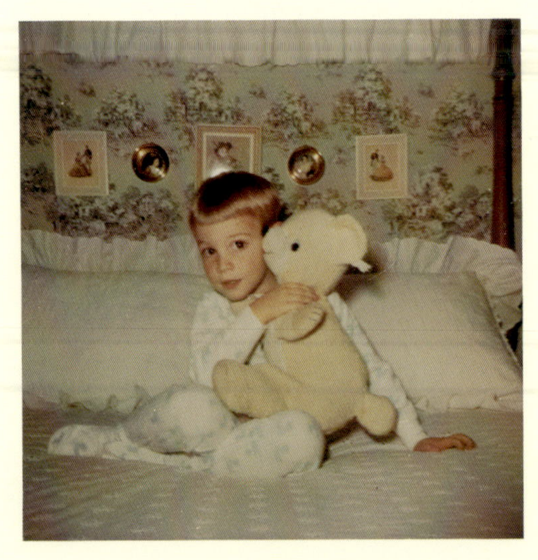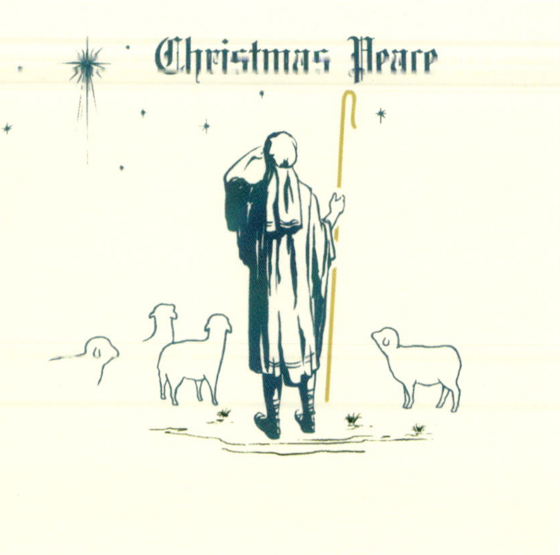
Christmas Peace

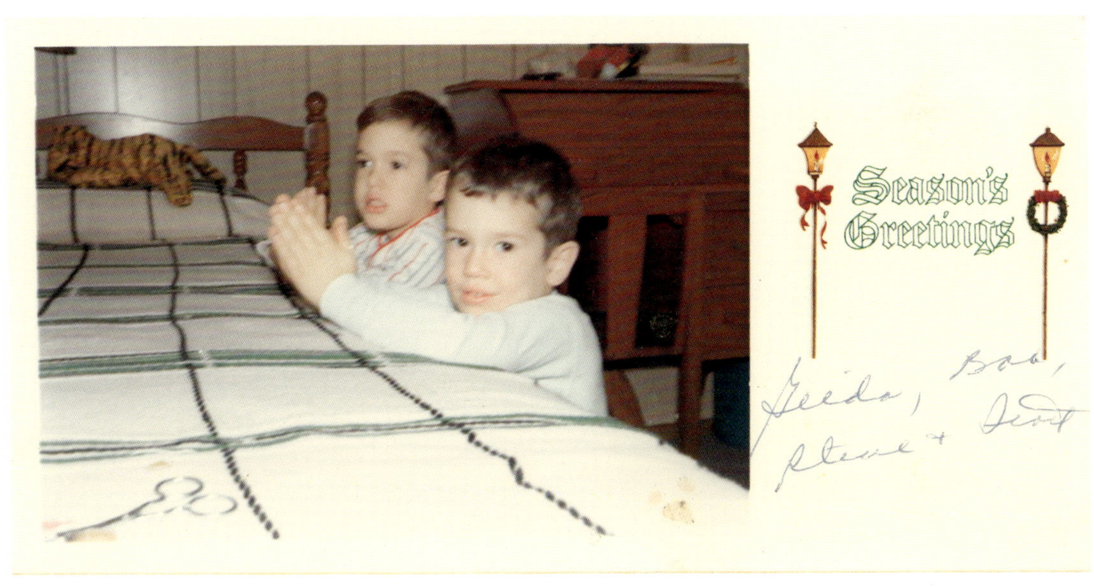

Season's
Greetings
Freida, Bob,
Steve & Scott

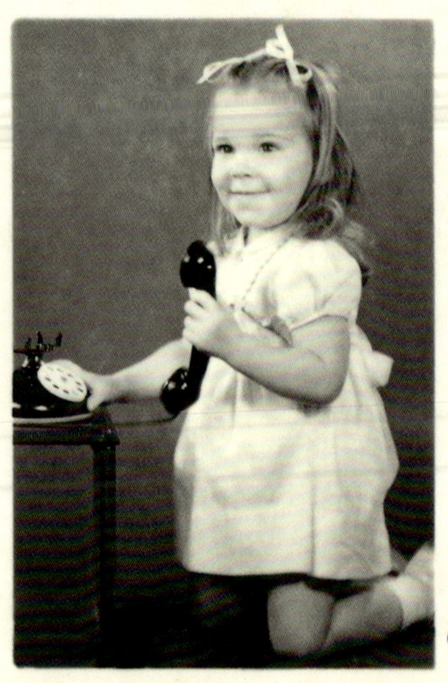

Merry Christmas

Edythe, Frank, and Meloa

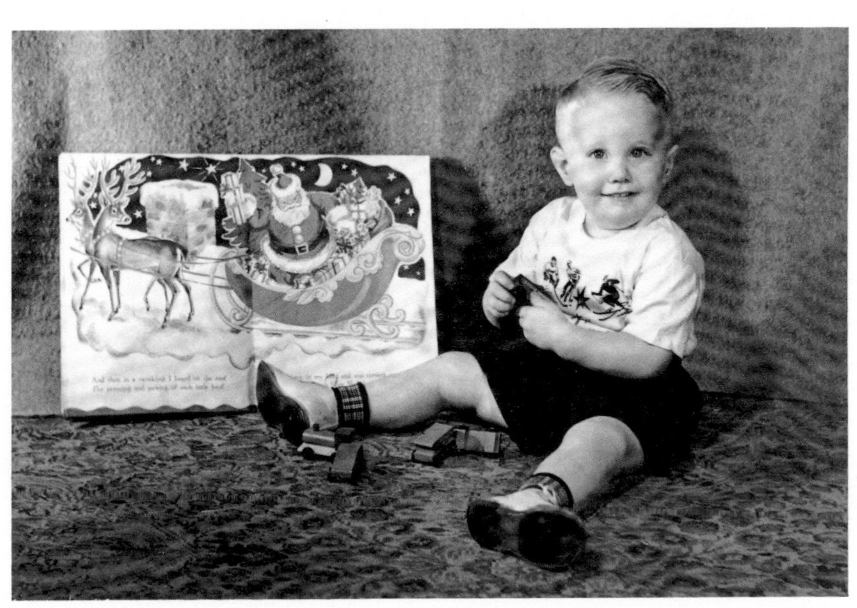

And then in a twinkling I heard on the roof
The prancing and pawing of each little hoof.

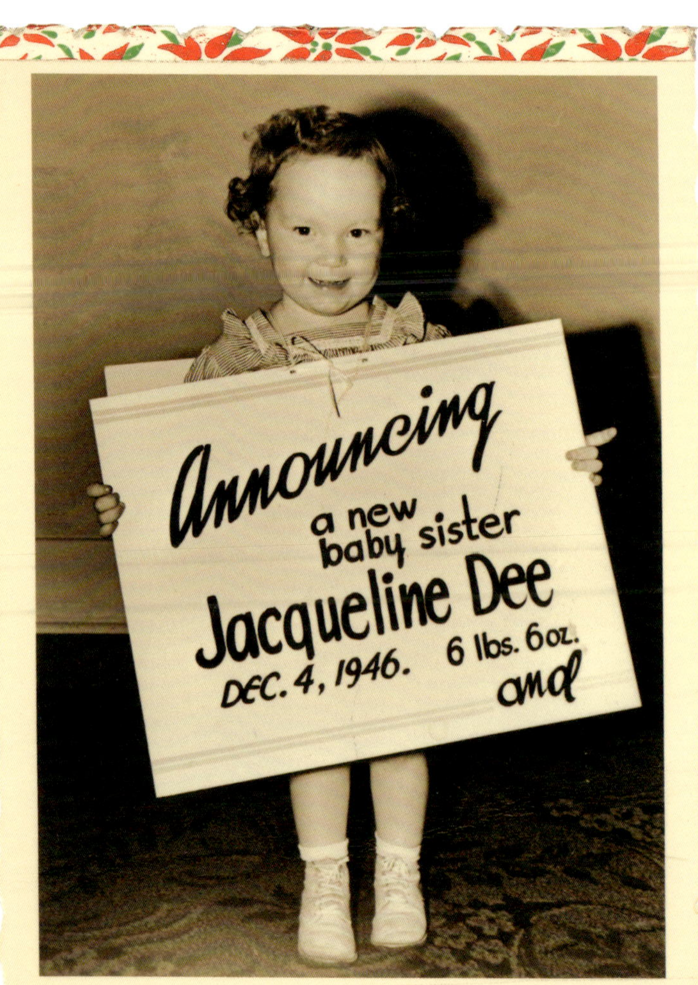
Announcing
a new
baby sister
Jacqueline Dee
DEC. 4, 1946.   6 lbs. 6 oz.

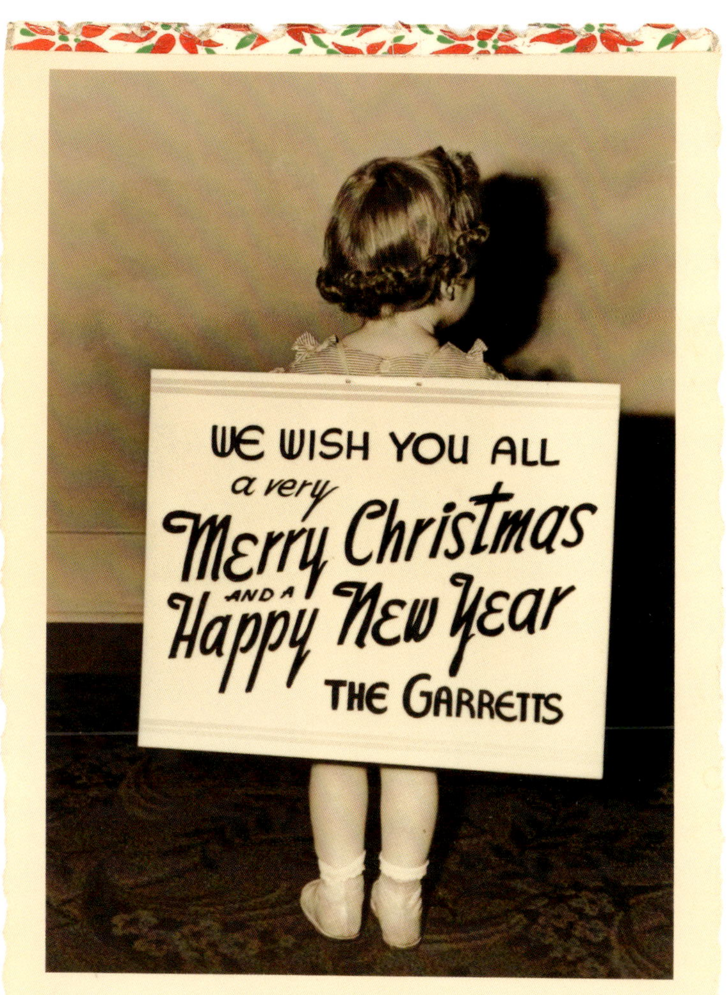

WE WISH YOU ALL
a very
Merry Christmas
AND A
Happy New Year
THE GARRETTS

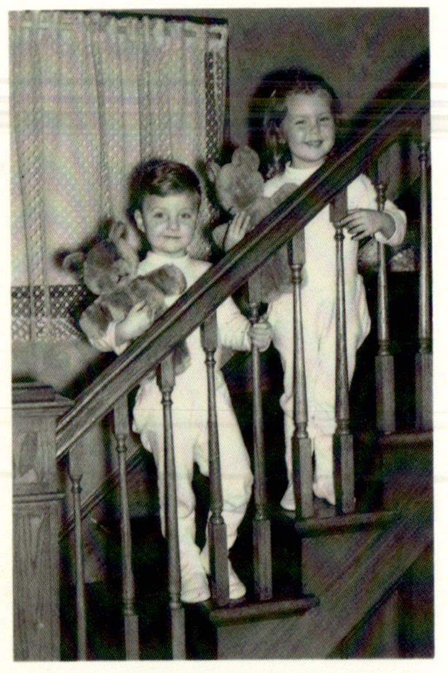

Best wishes for a

Merry Christmas

Jo, Buck and Twins

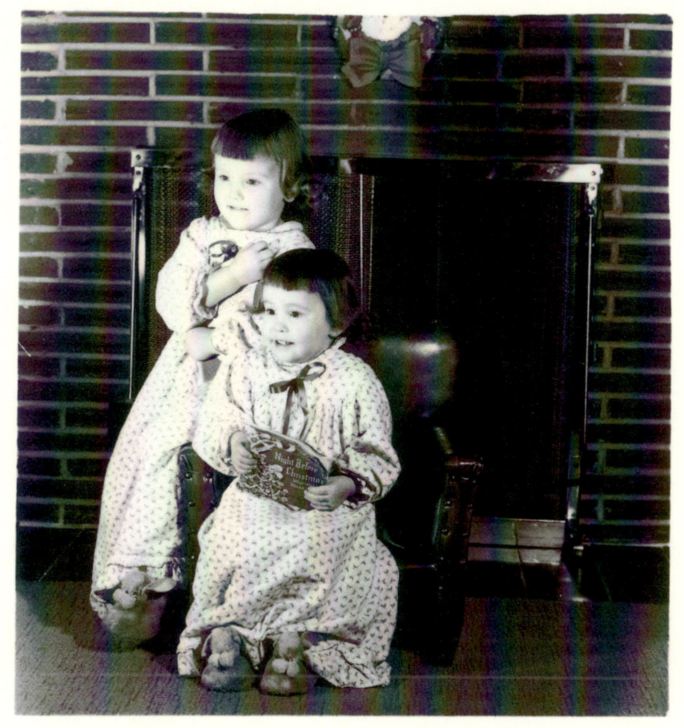

Season's Greetings

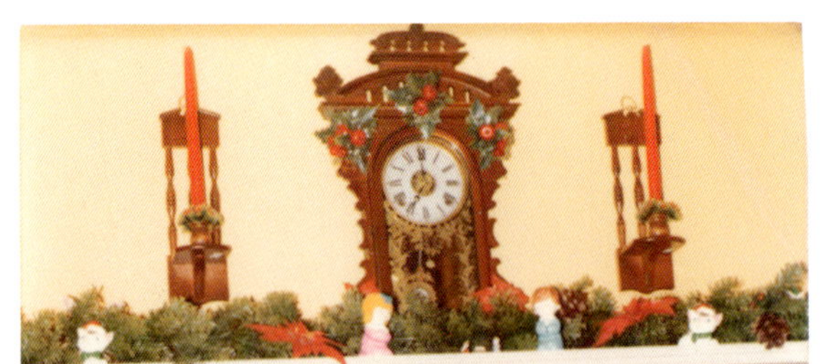

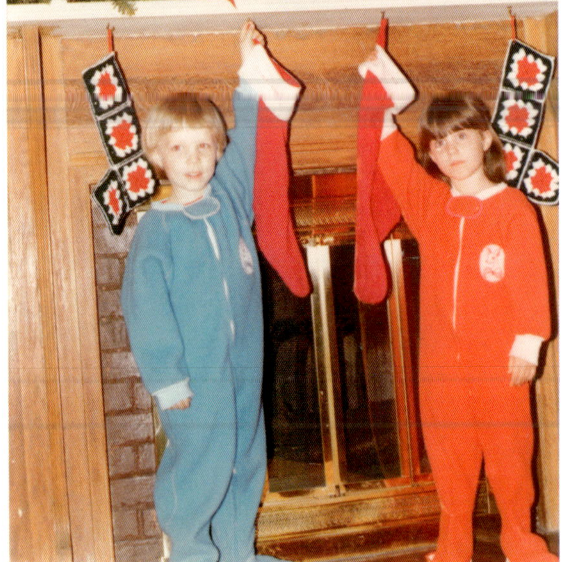

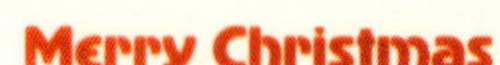

Merry Christmas

THE NIGHT BEFORE....
RICHARD, TEENA, TOM,
and ELEANOR CONKLIN

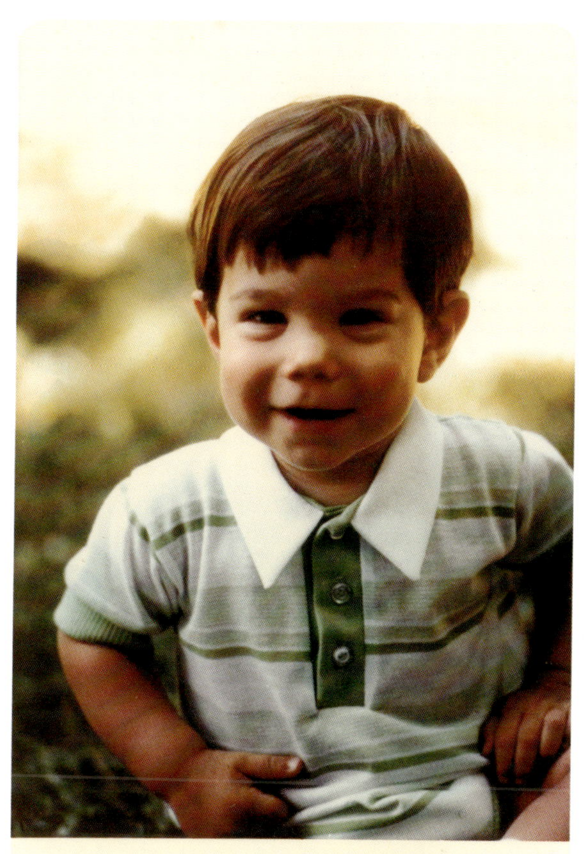

Peace on Earth

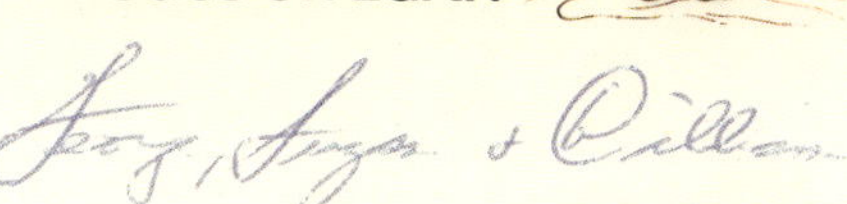

GREETINGS
FROM OUR HOUSE *
TO YOUR HOUSE *

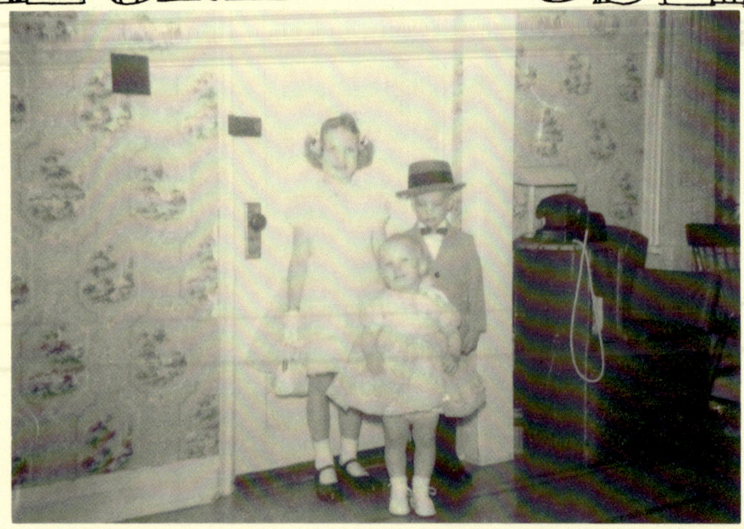

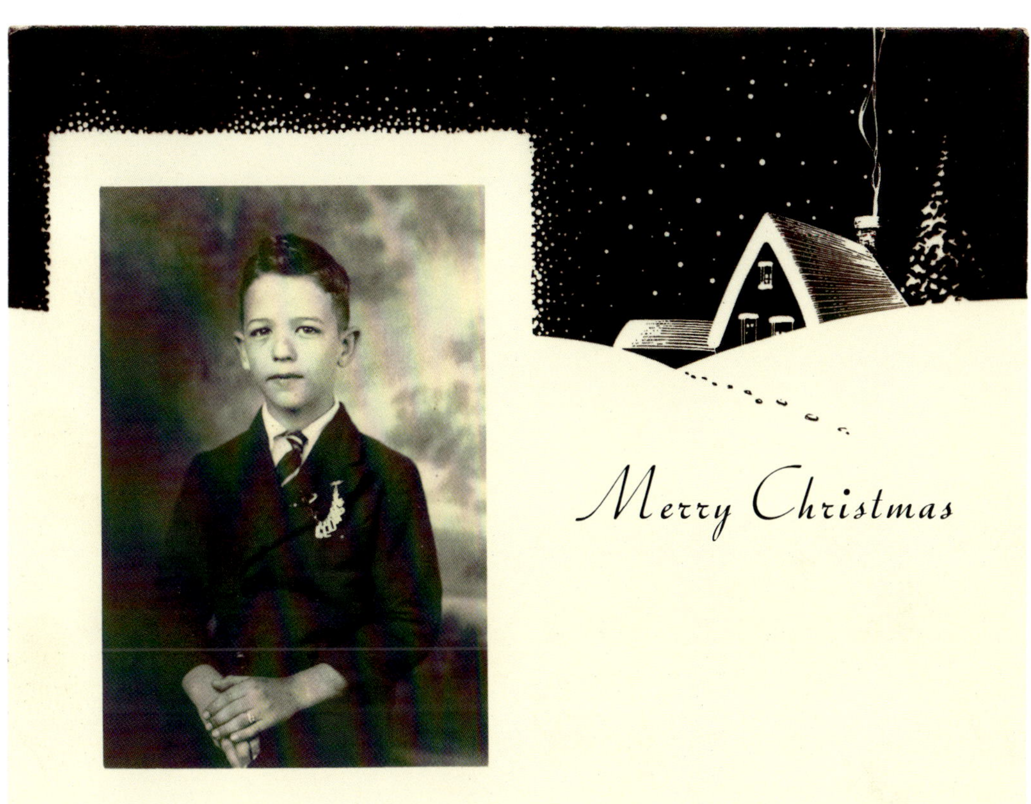

Merry Christmas

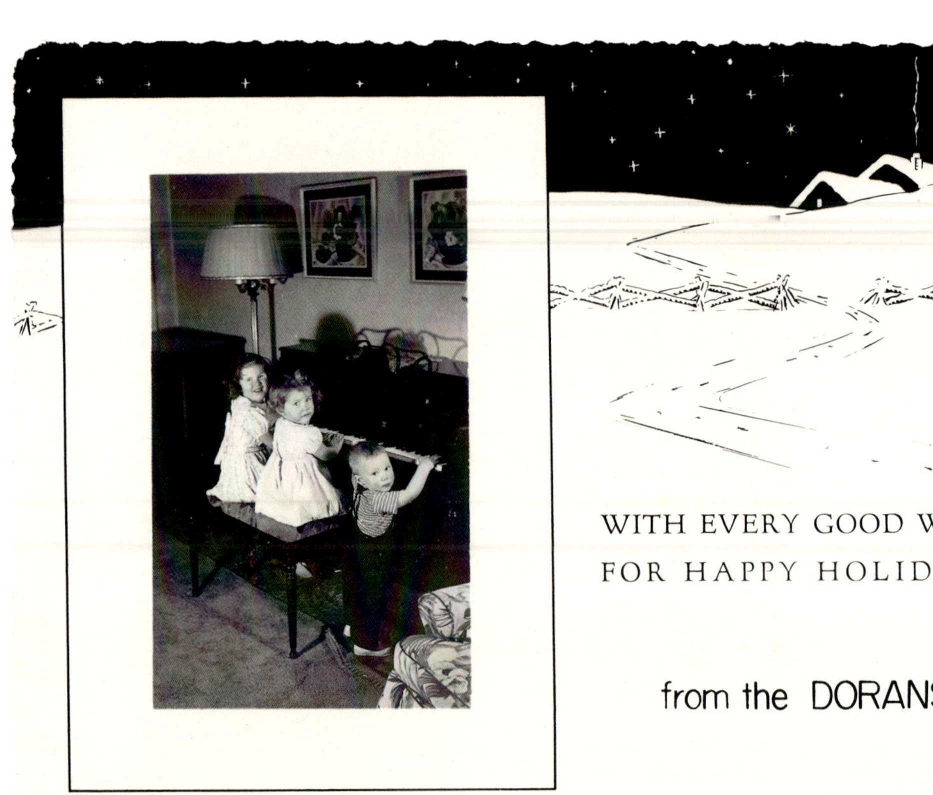

WITH EVERY GOOD WISH
FOR HAPPY HOLIDAYS

from the DORANS

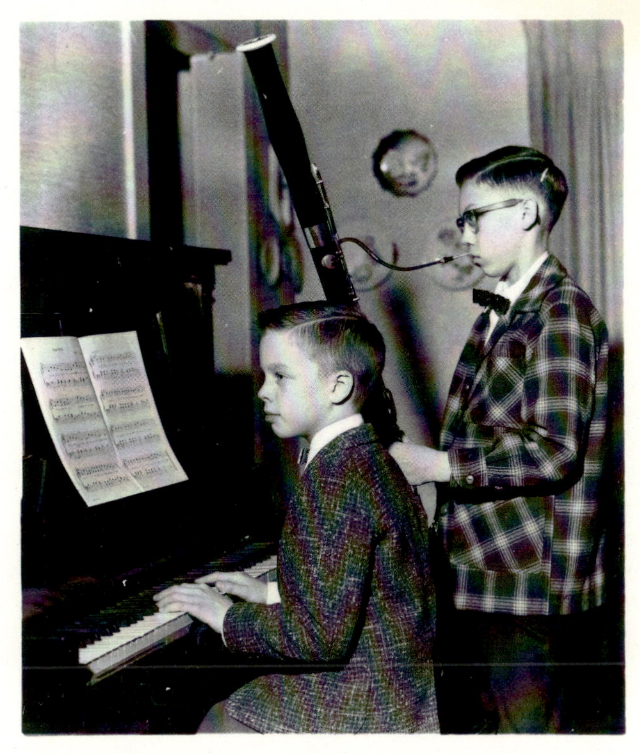

Season's Greetings

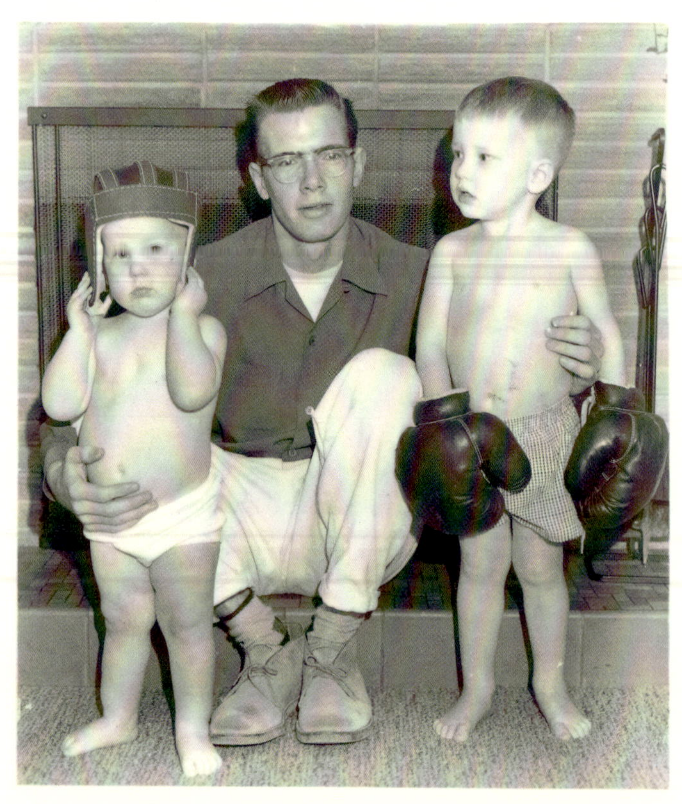

Season's Greetings

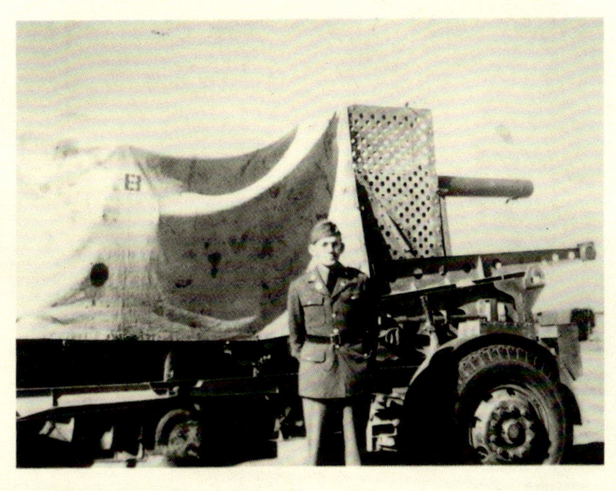

Wishing you a
Merry Christmas
and a Happy New Year!

Dec 25 - 1941

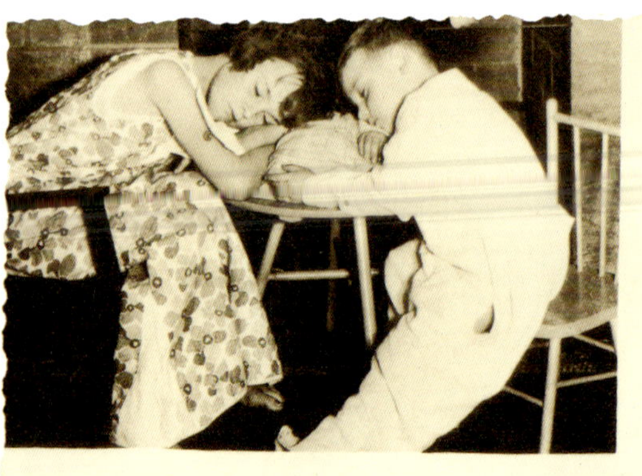

Time
Marches
On

1943

Christmas
Greetings
From The Bihlers
Same as
13 Years Ago

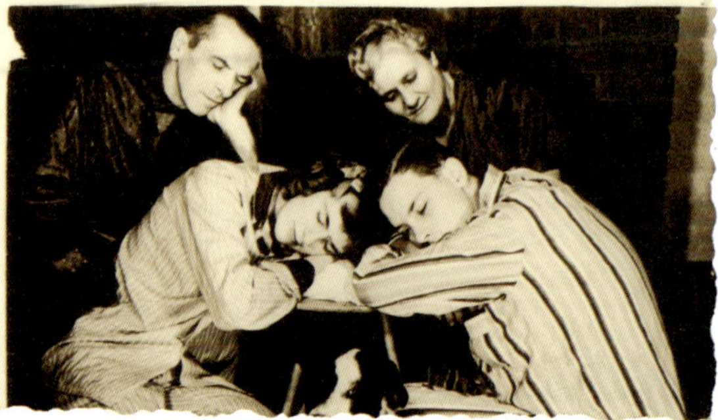

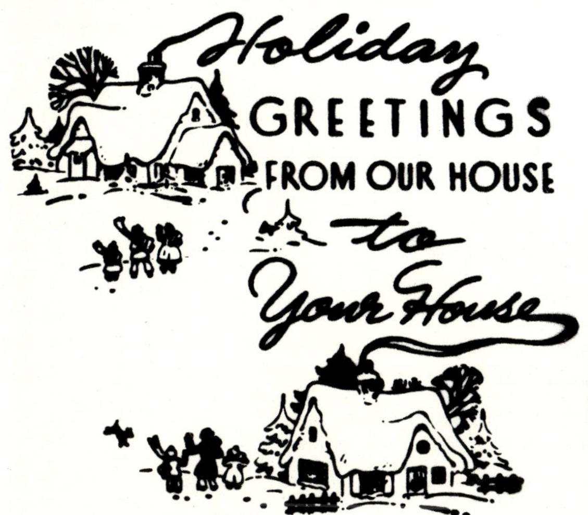

Holiday
GREETINGS
FROM OUR HOUSE
to
Your House

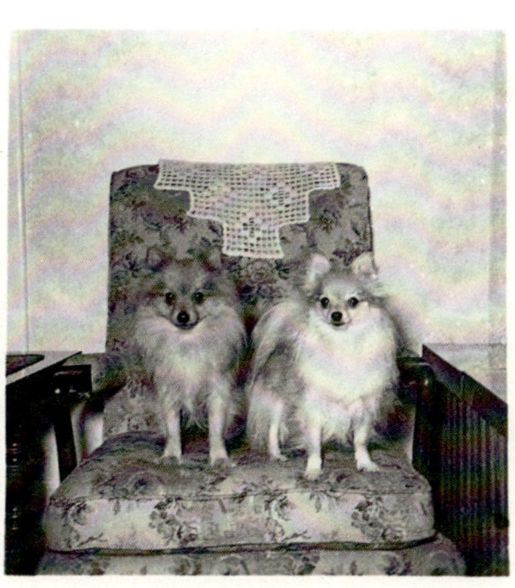

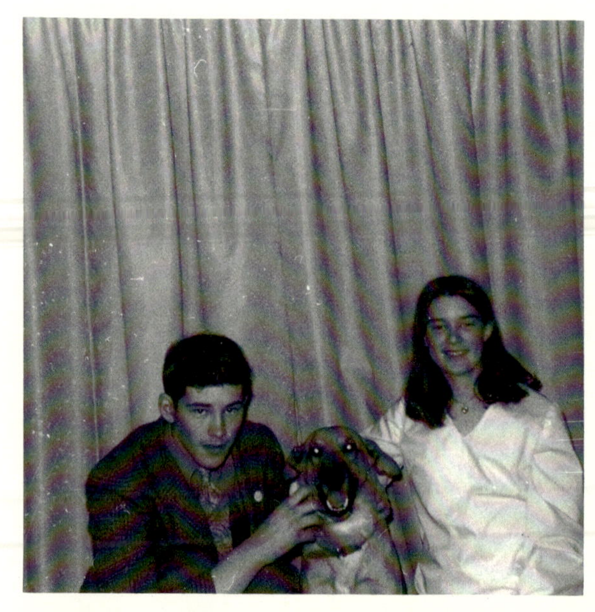

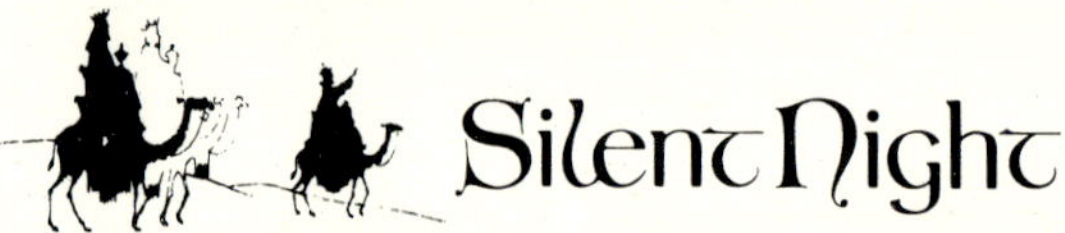
Silent Night

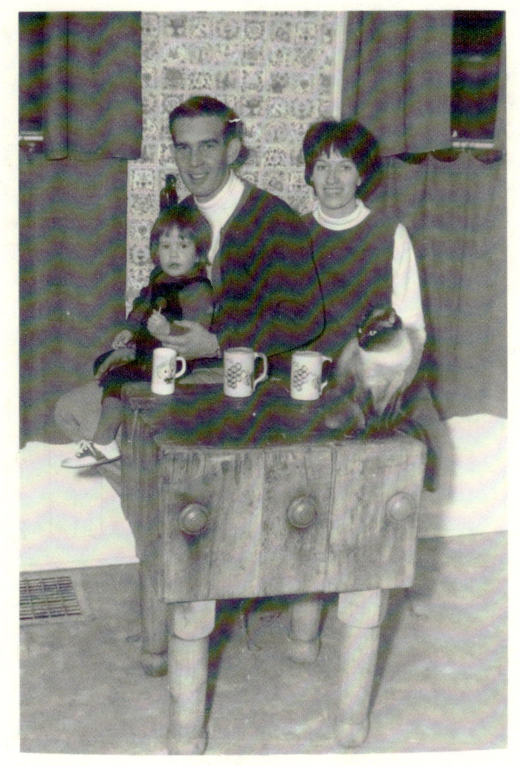

Nan

Bill

Amy

Tom

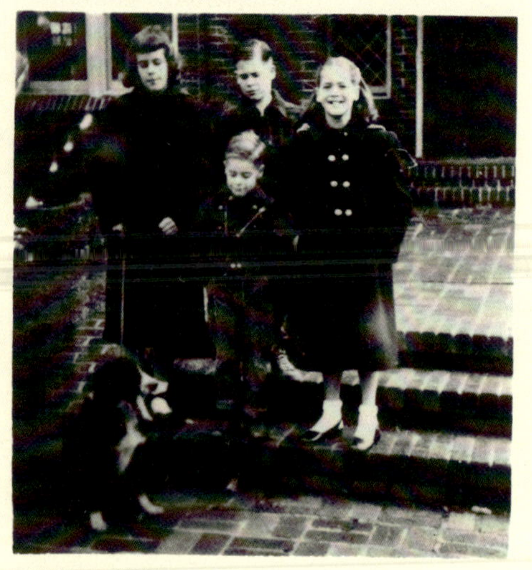

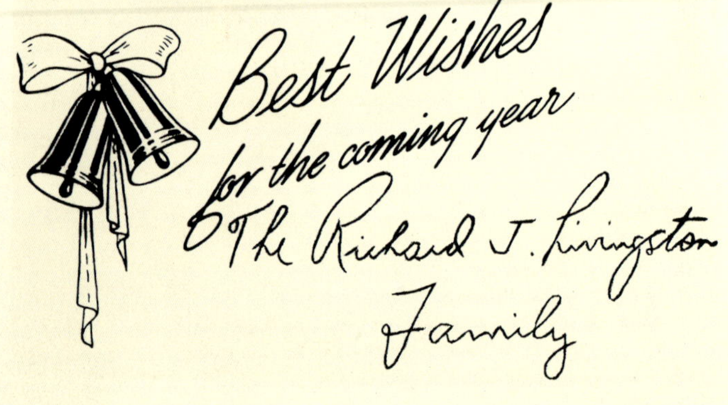
Best Wishes
for the coming year
The Richard J. Livingston
Family

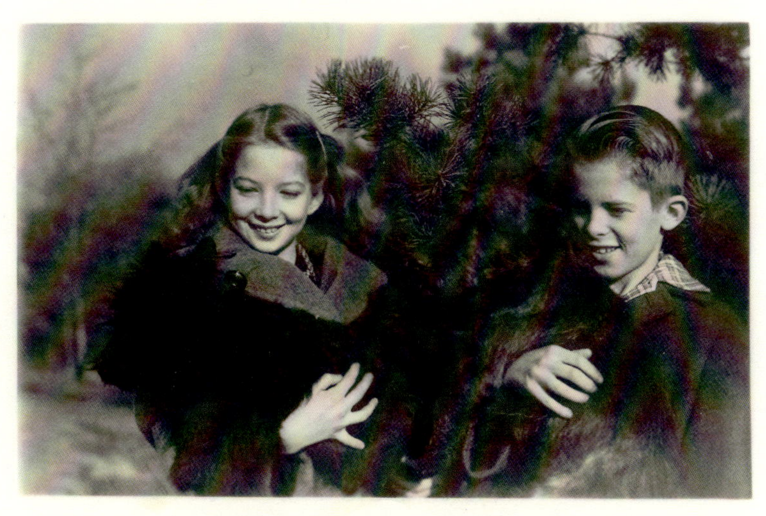

Merry Christmas

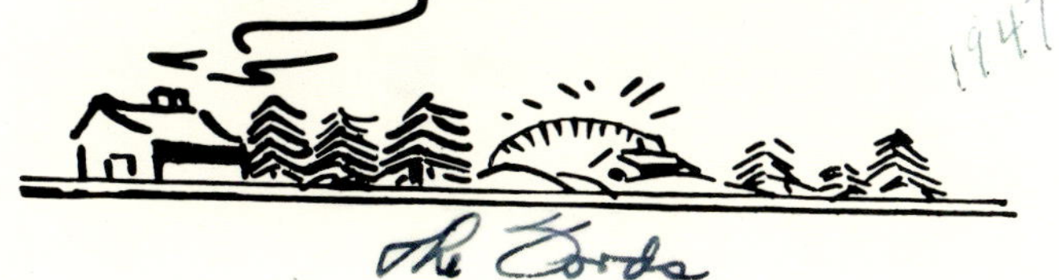

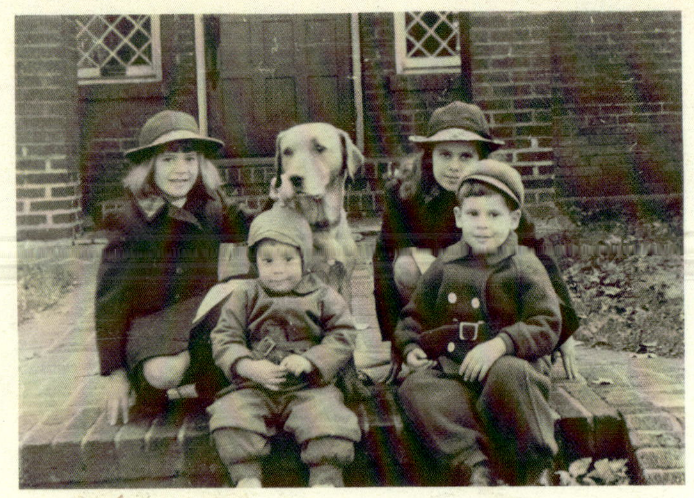

Merry
Christmas

1945

Richard J. Livingston Family

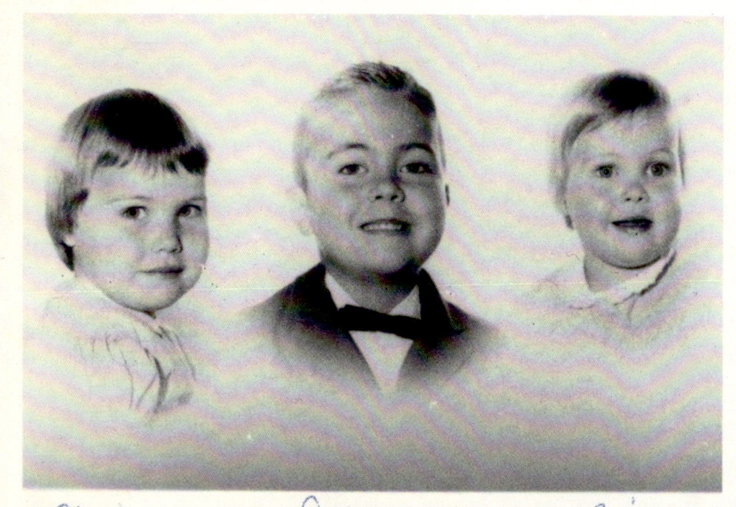

Elaine
3

Jeffrey
5

Lisa
18 mos.

Merry Christmas
Happy New Year

Jeanne and Ray Bradshaw over

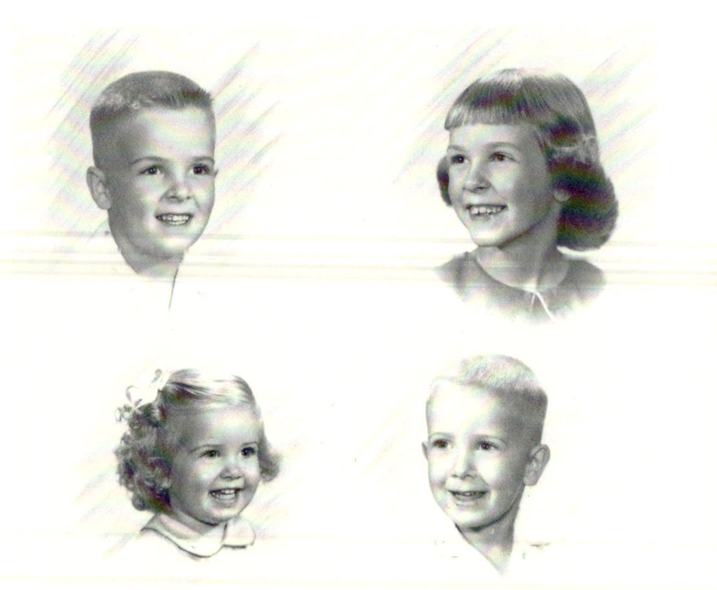

Season's Greetings

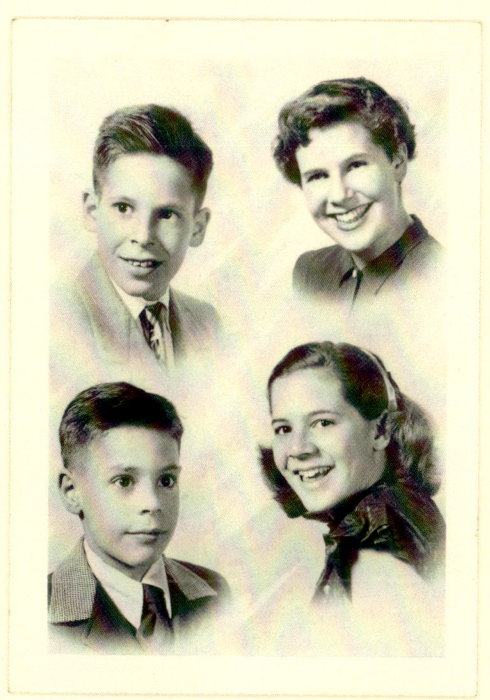

The Richard J. Livingston Family

1951

Season's Greetings

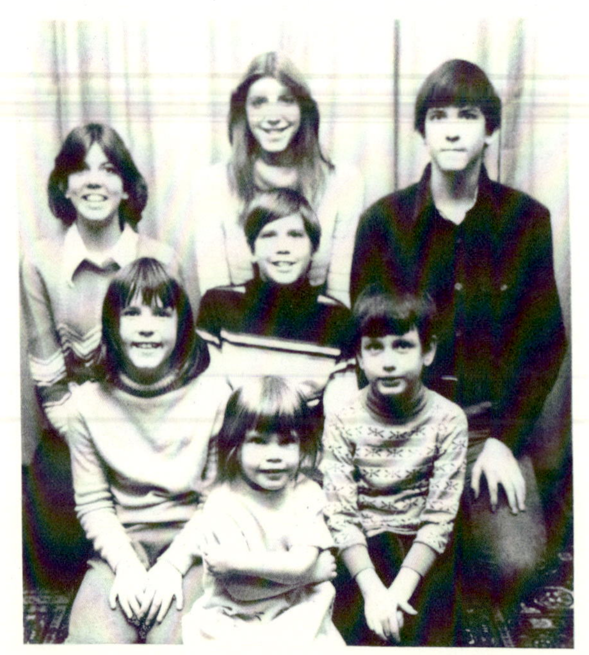

DEBBIE DEANNA DICK DAN DAURIE ANN DAVID DICKSIE

MERRILYN & DICK GIFFORD

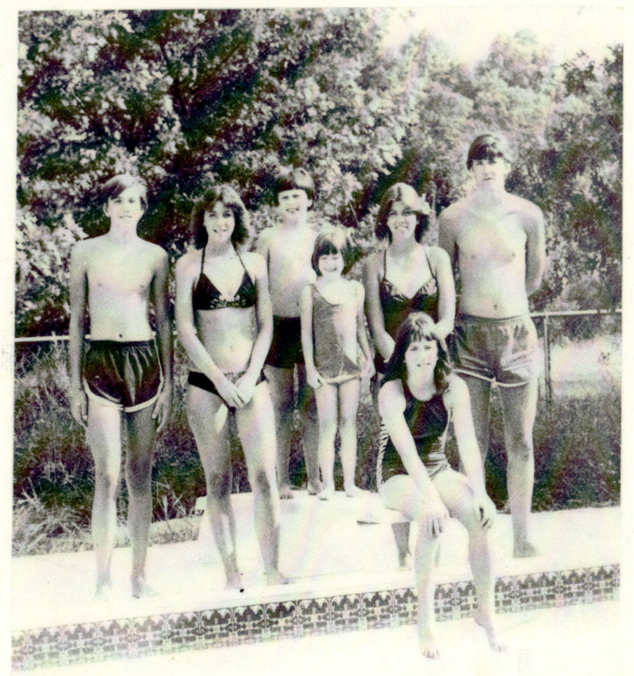

Season's Greetings
DEBBIE DEANNA DICK DAN DAURIE ANN DAVID DICKSIE
MERRILYN & DICK GIFFORD
1980

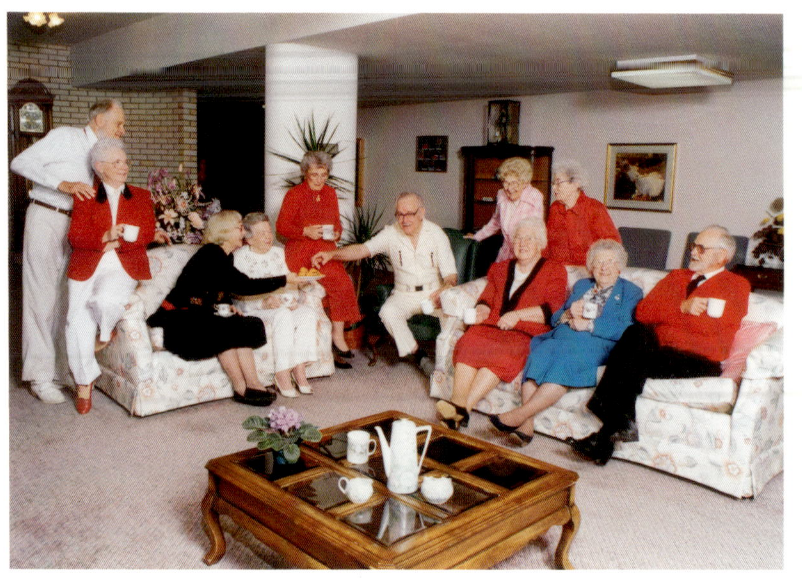

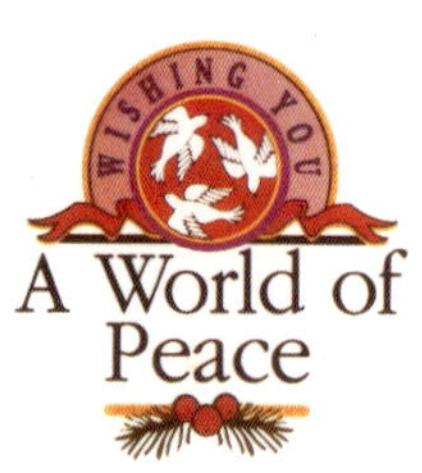

WISHING YOU
A World of
Peace

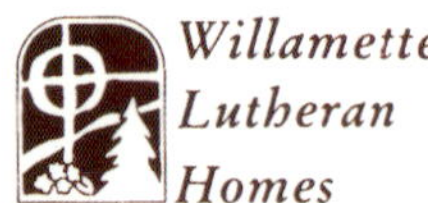

Willamette
Lutheran
Homes

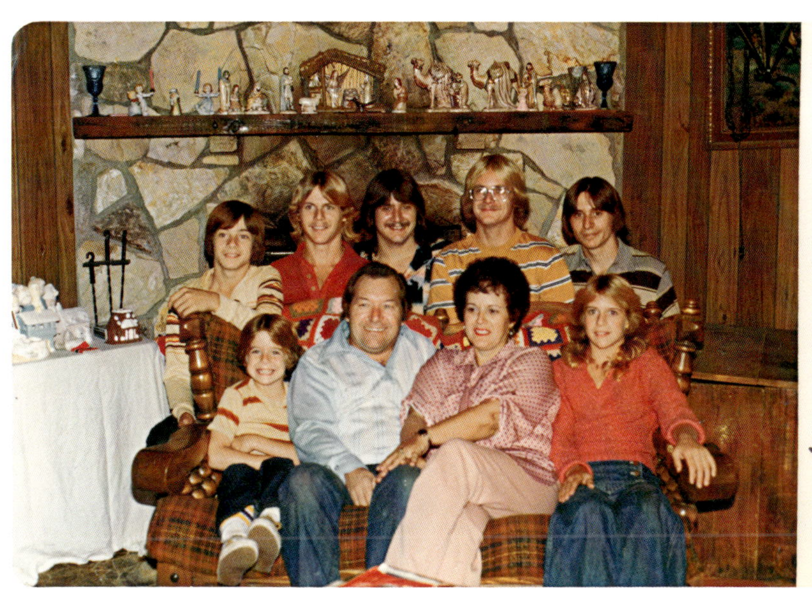

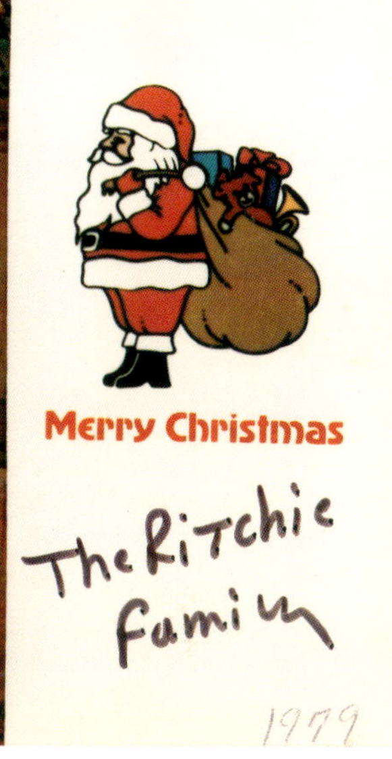

The Ritchie Family

1979

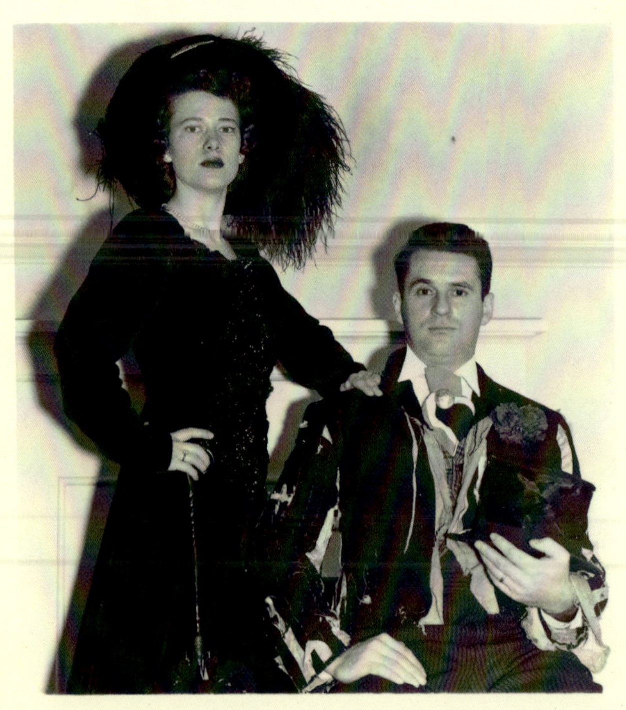

A Merry Christmas

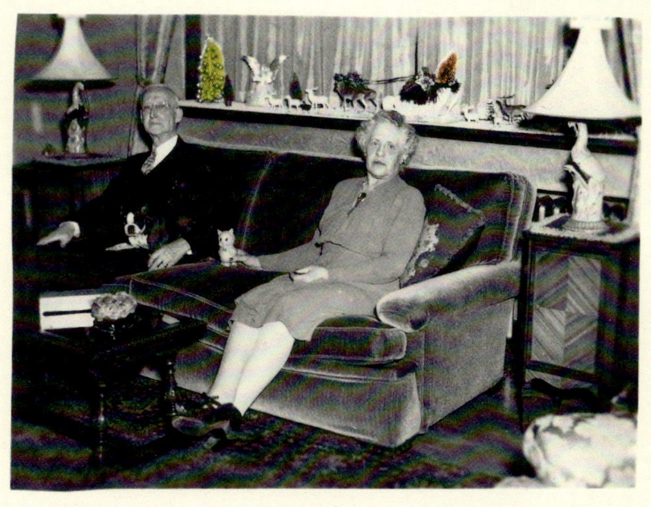

With sincere wishes for a

very Merry Christmas and a

Happy New Year

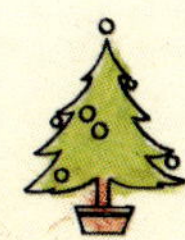

To the whole family,

Aunt Hattie & Uncle Abe.

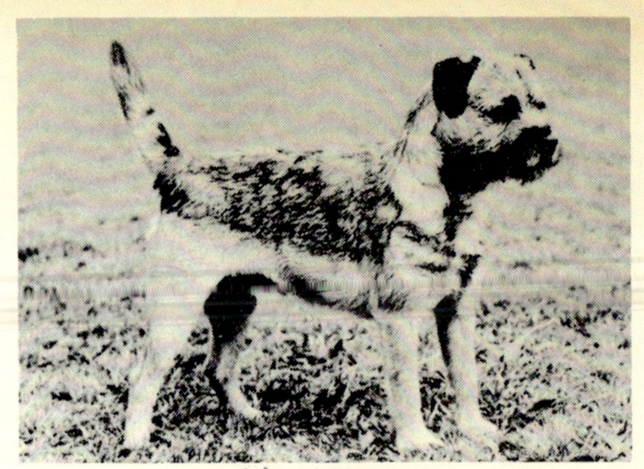

"Geordie"
Ch. Portholme Max Factor

Season's
Greetings

From
Dalquest

1954

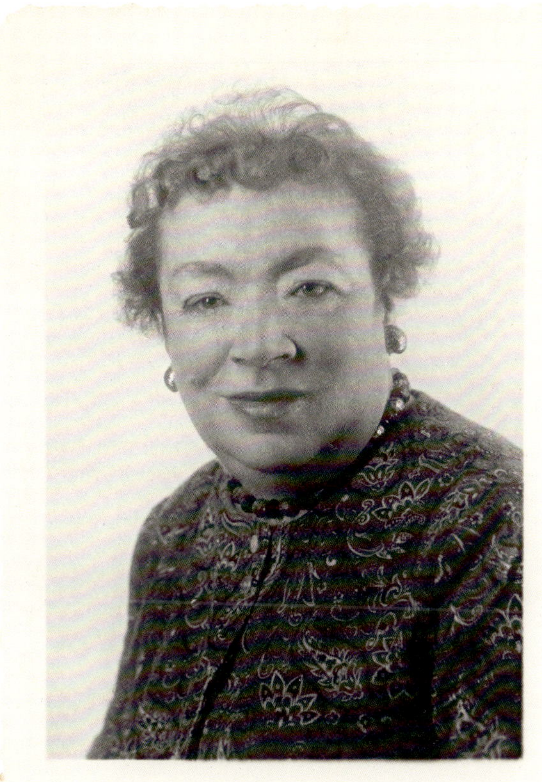

Merry Christmas

Happy New Year

1966

Love
Dottie

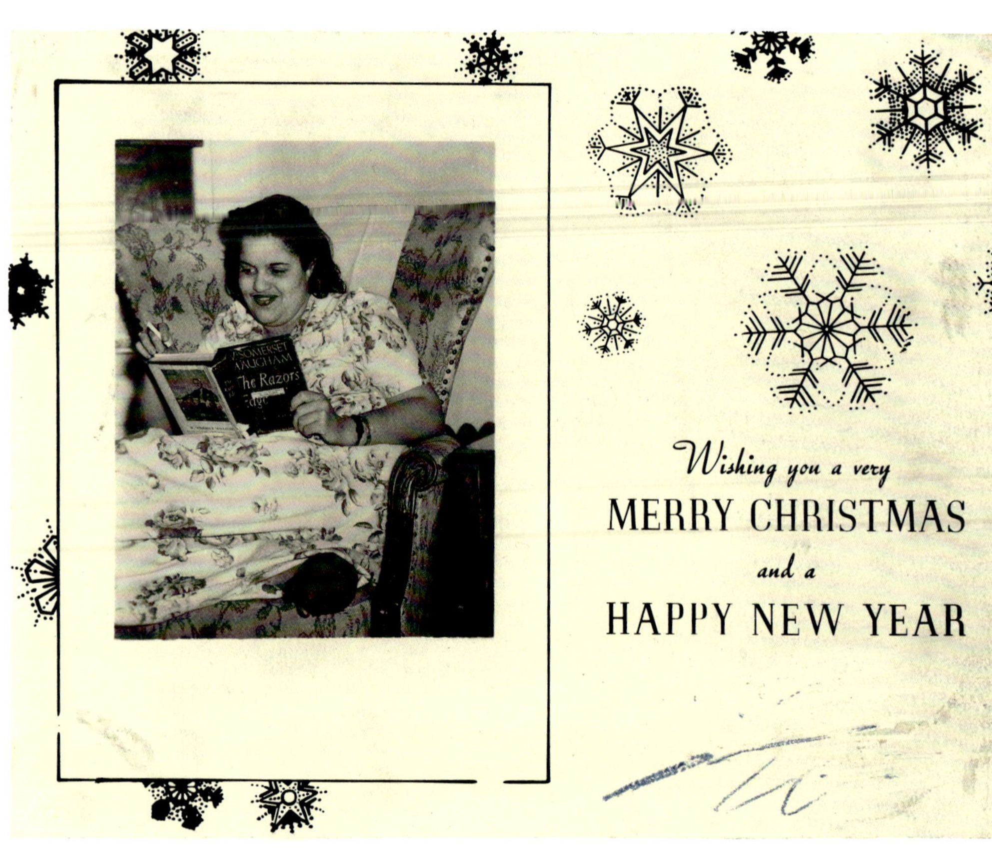

Wishing you a very
MERRY CHRISTMAS
and a
HAPPY NEW YEAR

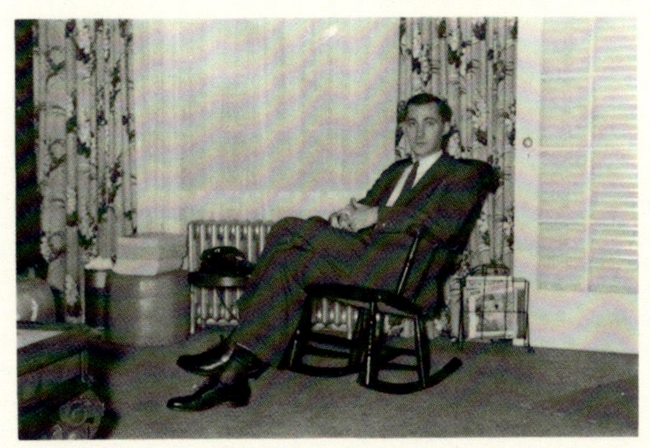

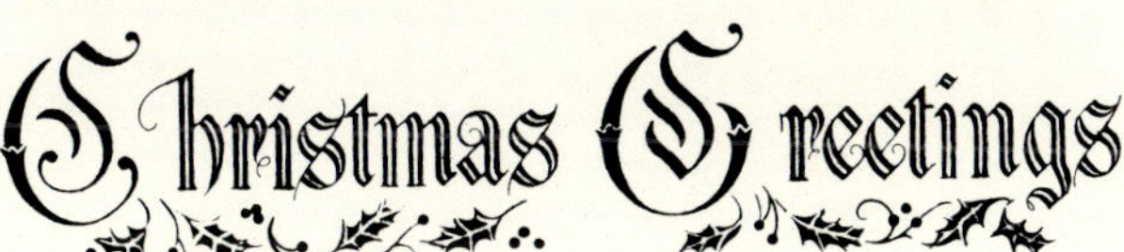
Christmas Greetings
AND BEST WISHES FOR THE NEW YEAR

merry Christmas

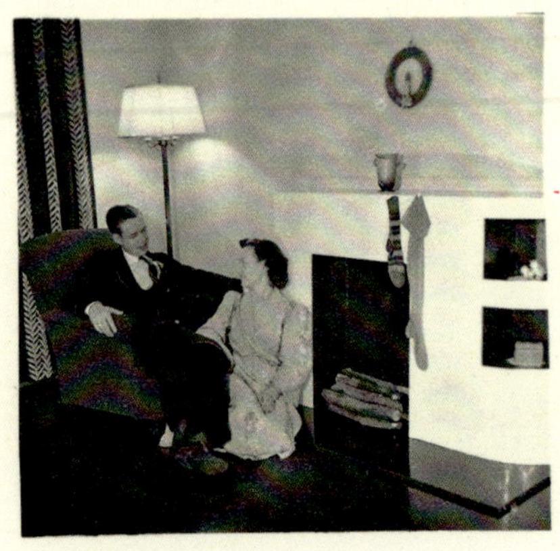

A. C. & Martha

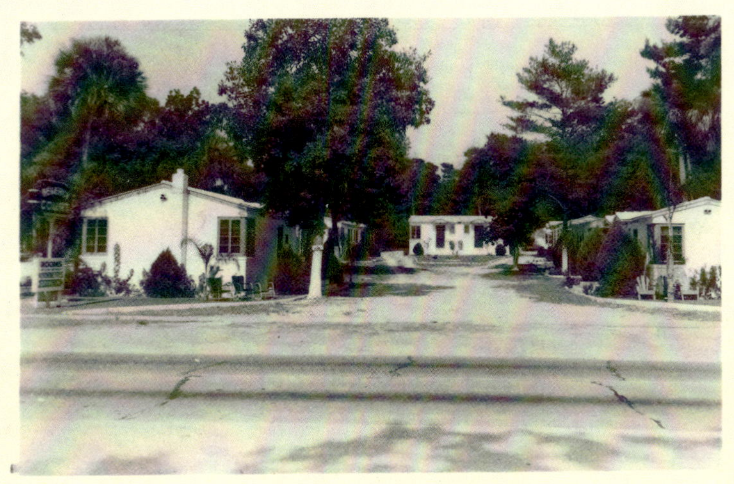

BEST WISHES FOR A

Merry Christmas

BEVERLY COURT
831 North Ridgewood Avenue
Holly Hill, Florida

COLLECTION MARTIN PARR